HERD-BOUND TO YOU!

How to reverse herd-bound behaviors
and get your horse focused on you

Teddie Ziegler

Author: Teddie Ziegler
Editor: Mark Mottershead
Design and Cover Art: Jose Pepito, Jr.
Photos: Bill Delaney
Subjects: Self-Help, Education; Adult education, Instructional, Horses

Disclaimer: The author makes no guarantees to the results you'll achieve by reading this book. All horse training requires know-how and persistence. The results and client case studies presented in this book represent results achieved working directly with the author. Your results may vary to these depending on your prior experience and application of the principles outlined.

This book is dedicated to my parents, Peter & Clara Ziegler. They bought me my first horse and supported my love of horses throughout my lifetime.

And to my precious horse, Apollo, who was my inspiration for writing this book.

CONTENTS

PREFACE

My goal with any of my training materials is to make you as self-sufficient a horse person as possible.

What I mean by that is I want you to be able to solve any issues that come up with your horse on your own so you don't need me or any other trainer ever again.

Now I know this is not the approach favored by most trainers as it cuts down on their ongoing revenue, but it's what I'd want from you if our positions were reversed.

More than that though, having studied and worked with several trainers myself, I've found that oftentimes they can only teach one part of the whole 'horse puzzle'.

Which means that sooner or later you have to go looking for another trainer to teach you the next piece of the puzzle with the result that you never really get to see the whole picture.

I want you to understand the whole picture.

I cannot guarantee that you will become totally independent just from reading this book but I do want you to be able to handle any and all issues that arise if you have a horse that is herd-bound.

That's my primary aim here, but I also have a secondary intention…

An early mentor of mine once told me, *"If you want people to believe you can help them, you'd better start off by actually helping them first."*

He called it getting **'Results in Advance'**.

I want you to get 'Results in Advance' from reading this book.

And when that happens and you resonate with my approach, my hope is that you will then want to continue your journey with horses with me, either through my online, self-study programs or through my personal coaching.

In fact, I'm going to tell you straight up here and now, I want to become the last trainer you'll ever need to go to or study with.

The reason I say this, apart from the goal of helping you become as self-sufficient as possible, is because of the results I have helped my students achieve that they've not been able to achieve before.

Here's what one of them recently told me:

> *"I felt like a failure as I couldn't get the results they (the other trainers) were getting. I felt like I was letting my horse down.*
>
> *"I knew I was missing something, that there were gaps. But I couldn't figure out how to bridge the gaps. The other trainers couldn't help me either.*
>
> *"But by reading your blogs and studying your work, I've started to be able to spot those gaps and fill them in and I'm getting results.*
>
> *"One thing that you do that is vital is explaining how the horse thinks, perceives and interprets what we are doing to him or asking of him.*

"Getting a physical response from the horse is not training unless the horse 'gets it' mentally and then willingly participates. Otherwise, it's just mindless motion."

My gift is being able to translate what your horse is saying to you and then help you become fluent in the same language.

This book is the first step in that transformation, so if you're ready, let's go!

How To Read This Book

In the Introduction Chapter that follows, I'll describe how I have classified the 3 stages of herd-bound behavior I've encountered so you can get an idea of where you are with your horse.

In Chapter 1 that follows I'll tell you my most recent case of herd-bound behavior which will hopefully help ease your concerns knowing that it can happen to any of us at any time - even with a horse I've known for over 30 years!

We will then get into the nuts and bolts of dealing with the issue. Regardless of which of the 3 stages you identify you're at, I suggest you read all 3 of the problem-solving chapters (2, 3, and 4) as they build upon each other. Plus they all contain slightly different ideas and suggestions and you may resonate with some concepts more than others.

Please note that throughout the book, I will be referring to the horse's gender as he or him to be consistent. This is primarily because all the horses I have owned in my adult life have been male but if your horse is a mare, please just replace those with she or her.

Your Safety

As always, my primary concern is for the safety and happiness of both you and your horse and I don't want to see anybody get hurt.

Since I'm unable to work with you and your horse in person, you should already have a strong foundation on how to handle your horse from the ground and how to keep yourself safe when around your horse.

You must already have basic horsemanship skills and have the ability to move your horse away from you easily, at any speed. This will protect you in many situations.

I may also advise you sometimes to use a reed or a whip to help you keep your horse at a safe distance. However, please do not take this as a recommendation to hit your horse. I never hit a horse in my care. Rather, these items are for you to use as tools (extensions of your body) to create a larger, protective bubble around yourself.

If the questions being asked of you by your horse are not matched by your experience level or your ability with horses, then I always recommend that you seek outside help from someone more experienced than yourself, rather than going at it alone.

In addition, if you are not achieving the results you want or you sense that there is a chance either you or your horse could get hurt, then stop and seek direct help from a suitably qualified instructor or you can book a consultation with me here:

https://teddiezieglerhorsemanship.com/book-call/

Following on from this, we'd better deal with all the necessary legal stuff.

Legal Disclaimer

Equine training can be a hazardous activity, which may result in serious injury and/or death.

This book provides general information, instructions, and techniques, which may not be suitable for everyone or every horse.

I can therefore make no warranty or representation and assume no liability concerning the validity of any advice, opinion, demonstration, or recommendation expressed within.

You must rely on this material at your own risk.

I am sharing my experiences with you so that they may help you as they have helped me.

Furthermore, I shall have neither liability for, nor responsibility to, any person or entity with respect to any loss or damage caused or alleged to be caused, directly or indirectly, by the information contained within this book.

Your Agreement

By continuing to retain or read this book, you give your tacit agreement to the above Legal Disclaimer.

Should you not wish to do so, then please write and let me know via my Support Desk (help.teddiezieglerhorsemanship. com) and I will authorize an immediate refund for you.

INTRODUCTION

*"Change the way you look at things and
the things you look at change."*
WAYNE DYER

How do I stop my horse from being herd-bound?

Is one of the most frequently asked questions I get from my blog readers and students. Because of this, I wanted to share my personal experiences of dealing with herd-bound horses in this book. My goal is to help as many horse owners and enthusiasts as possible overcome this vexing issue.

There are three types of severity I have found in herd-bound horses and have developed easy-to-follow protocols for each. My approach when facing any issue with horses is to always *'Push the Easy Button'*. So I am confident that the solutions I will be sharing with you in this book will work for you and your horse as well.

Herd-bound behaviors in a horse can range from annoying to dangerous. So let me give you a quick overview of my definition of the three levels of herd-bound behaviors that I have dealt with:

Mild Cases

Your horse may not want to leave his buddy but will once you have him haltered. This could be classified as an annoyance. It means your horse is hard to catch, hard to halter and isn't always reliable when you have him on a lead rope. He may stop and start, whinny to go back, not pay attention to you, or pull on the lead rope. These behaviors can be frustrating and can get in the way of training.

Is this where you are?

Medium Cases

Your horse may exhibit all the above behaviors but be more aggressive. So the pulling on the lead rope can turn into bolting and running back to the other horse. Your horse may start pawing the ground. Since he's not paying attention to you, he may accidentally hit you with his front leg or step on your foot. This now goes beyond the point of frustration and moves to being unsafe. This becomes more of a roadblock when it comes to training.

Sometimes the aggressive behavior gets worse as the horse is taken further away. I've even seen horses bite their owners while being groomed because they left their buddy.

When he sees you with a halter, he might decide to run around the pasture to keep away from you. I've seen horses strike out or try to kick their owners while tacking up.

In medium cases, riding might even become dangerous. I've seen horses grudgingly do what their owners want when haltered but then immediately act out once mounted. I've seen horses throw their owners off because all they wanted to do was to get back to their buddy in the pasture

Perhaps you have experienced some of these behaviors from your horse.

Severe Cases

If a horse has a severe case of being herd-bound then he may run around full blast in the pasture to try to get away from a halter and may end up hurting himself. Without a care for his own safety, he can damage his stifle or even fracture a leg. If you are in the pasture with that horse, he may not hesitate to run you over if you get in his way. So in a worst-case scenario, both you and your horse could be in danger of a serious injury.

The stress and anxiety caused by a severe case of herd-bound behavior can also lead to colic. If any of these injuries happen, then emotional trauma and fear memories will be created right before your eyes as well. This can turn into a serious issue and be hard to resolve except for the most experienced.

Here are some more signs and symptoms...

(We are only talking about a situation where two horses are in the same pasture together.)

<u>In a mild case, your horse may do some or all of these things</u>:

- Whinny and constantly look for the other horse when he is taken out of the pasture.
- Walk along the fence line watching the other horse as he leaves.

- Stop grazing and wear a pathway down in the pasture waiting for the other horse to return.
- Paw at the gate to get out to be with the other horse.
- Continually stand at one location where he can see the other horse and whinny to him intermittently.

Or, when you take him out, your horse may do some or all of these things:

- Pull on the lead to watch where his buddy is in the pasture.
- Try to turn around and go back to the pasture a few times.
- Stop and whinny to his buddy still in the pasture.
- Not pay close attention to you but still do what you ask, kind of.
- After a short session/lesson, he will stand at the arena gate pushing on it telling you he is done. You can tell he wants to go back to the pasture with his buddy. He will then continue the session/lesson when you ask but then go back over to the gate over and over.

In a medium case, your horse may do some or all of these things:

- Whiny all the time and push on the fence or the gate to try to get out.
- Trot constantly, going back and forth along the fence line and whinnying to the other horse.
- Run around the pasture looking for the other horse and working up a sweat.
- Come over to you (when the other horse is gone) but then trot away. Then he will come back over to you as if to ask you to take him out too and then run off again.

- Let you halter him but then trot quicker than you can walk and get ahead of you, trying to get to the gate in a hurry.

Or, when you take him out, your horse may do some or all of these things:

- Pull away from you and bolt back to the pasture to be with his buddy.
- Continue to pull on the lead and shake his head in frustration.
- Stomp on the ground and snort as you try to lead him away from the pasture.
- Not listen to you in the arena during a session/lesson and ignore you looking to find a way to get back to his buddy.
- Do what you ask in the session/lesson but then go over to the gate to say, "Okay, we're done," and refuse to continue the session/lesson.
- Shake his head, act up, crow hop, and not listen to you while riding.

In a severe case, your horse may do some or all of these things:

- Run constantly back and forth along the fence line and whinny to the other horse.
- Have no regard for anyone or anything else in the pasture with him.
- Be frantic, panicked, white-eyed, and/or work up a frothy sweat.
- While trotting or running, shake his head, kick out, and/ or rear.

- Not let you halter him, touch him, get close, or calm him down.

Or, when you take him out, your horse may do some or all of these things:

- If you can catch him, he won't stop moving around you and circles you at a trot.
- Rear up or crow hop as you try to take him to the arena.
- Kick out at you while you're leading him.
- Pin his ears and try to bite you while you're leading him.
- Not give you his attention in the arena and run around the arena with no regard for you, just trying to get out.
- Rear up or buck to throw you off if you are riding in order to get back to the other horse.

This is only a general overview of my signs and symptoms list. If your horse does any of these things or more, he is showing signs and symptoms of being herd-bound. Whichever case you and your horse are in now, I have a solution for you.

The solutions that I discuss have all worked for me and my clients for many years. They are my tried-and-true fixes for this specific problem. I sincerely hope that one of them works to resolve your herd-bound issues with your horse.

I am sharing these solutions with you in this short book because I want to help you. I've heard people say that they've just given up and sold their horse due to herd-bound issues. I don't want to see that happen for both you and your horse's sake.

Note: Even though these solutions have worked for me and others, I'm sure there is a horse out there that none of these *solutions work for. If this is the case, then I suggest mixing it up and trying a bit of each tip, using trial and error while you work with your horse. Pay close attention to when something is working and what isn't. Then stick with the pieces that are helping your horse and continue from there.*

Another suggestion is to start with the easy answer and ramp up from there, going from the mild solution to the medium solution. Then if you need to, go to the severe solution.

As you read the book, you may think there is a lot of repetition but as the old saying goes, repetition is the mother of all learning.

It may also seem at times that I am asking you to do a lot of doing not very much but trust the process because there is a very definite method to the apparent madness, as you will discover.

If you don't follow the steps exactly as I have them laid out, it definitely won't work. You will be setting yourself up for your own failure. So, please trust the process and follow the steps properly. You'll be excited to see the end results.

And if all the above and what you are about to read in the coming chapters still don't work for you, then I want you to contact me so we can chat one-to-one to find a solution that does work for you.

This is a complimentary call because I truly want to help you resolve this issue with your horse. I know how frustrating it can be. You will be able to book a call with me by clicking the following link or visiting my website:

https://teddiezieglerhorsemanship.com/book-call/

Before we get into the nitty-gritty, I'd like to tell you a little about me as I think it will help put into context everything you are about to learn.

About Me

My name is Teddie Ziegler, and like everyone else, I am a blend of my parents in both personality and heritage. Because of that, I feel very blessed. My father was a research psychologist for the government, and I got my love of research from him. He is also a kind and gentle man who is always willing to help anyone in need.

My mother was a social worker with a heart of gold. She always went the extra mile to help someone out, no matter what their situation. My mother is where I get my bleeding heart, my love of animals, and my strong will to help the underdog.

In my case, it has become all about helping give horses a voice. I also enjoy helping their owners understand them better. The goal is to develop the relationship and performance of their dreams for both the human and the horse.

I got my first horse when I was six years old, a little Shetland pony called Farnley's Notable. He came home with me after being abandoned by his owner. He lived in my parents' garage until we could build a barn in our backyard. He was my first rescue horse, but not my last.

Like most horse-crazy little girls, I spent as much time around horses as I could. I competed in many English disciplines. I won ribbons and trophies in jumping, English pleasure, show hunter, and classical dressage. I did this all as a child and as a young adult.

As idyllic as my childhood sounds, it wasn't always like that.

I've been through several traumatic experiences which have not only shaped my life but greatly impacted my approach with horses.

I suffered trauma and abuse as both a child and a young adult but my horses (Farnley, Tinkerbell, and Honey) helped me heal through the years. As a result, I have always wanted to give back to horses what they have so graciously provided me: healing, trust, and protection.

To this day, I especially resonate with the plight of rescue horses and I'm sure it's because of the trauma and abuse we both share.

I'm originally from Maryland and went to Towson University after leaving high school, where I earned a bachelor's degree and a master's degree in behavioral psychology.

Family is very important to me and as my parents had decided to retire in California, I moved out there to be with them a few years after graduation.

I worked for one of the nation's leading mental health facilities helping with autistic children and elderly patients, and later became a private therapist for Alzheimer's patients.

My first love though has always been horses and so after studying with some of the top names in the horse industry, I became a trainer myself.

I purchased a quarter horse who had been trained in cutting. This was Jazz. I tried to do English disciplines with him, but he obviously preferred Western, so I went with the flow (HINT: one of my 'secrets') and schooled with some wonderful Western-disciplined trainers. Jazz taught me a lot himself as well.

We ended up competing together in Western equitation, Western pleasure, cutting, and team penning. We had a blast and were a really good team together.

I bred Jazz, who sired Apollo, and apart from a brief period (a story for another day), the three of us spent the next 31 years together until Jazz passed away at the age of 34 in 2020. Apollo followed not long after in mid-2021 when he died of a heart attack during a severe tornado that came through the farm. I miss them both to this day.

In 2016 I had acquired another horse, D'Artagnan, who I quickly discovered was my soul horse. So as you can imagine, I was shattered when he unexpectedly passed away from a brain aneurysm in 2020. You can read about it here:

https://teddiezieglerhorsemanship.com/
forever-loving-home-for-horses/

I have learned so much from these guys over the years, as well as my other three horses growing up. It has truly been an extraordinary privilege to have been in their lives, and I owe them a huge debt of gratitude. They will all hold a special place in my heart forever.

I'm delighted to report though that a new horse entered my life a few months ago (at the time of writing) and you can follow Merlin's progress starting here:

https://teddiezieglerhorsemanship.com/a-gift-from-jazz/

Over the years I have taught a lot of courses. I've taught basic horsemanship, safety around horses, relationship and behavioral training, liberty and groundwork. I have also given riding lessons to both adults and children. Yet it has always intrigued me why some people get results while others don't and why some horses react in certain ways and others are completely the opposite.

After a while I started studying equine science and doing research like my father had done. What I discovered surprised me, as it often went against much of what we are taught about horses.

I added these findings to my own personal experiences, my knowledge of behavioral psychology from my university days, and blended all that with my mother's compassionate heart-guided ways to come up with my own unique approach to training horses. I hope you like it!

I always want to allow horses to have a voice and allow them to take part in the conversation. This has always felt right to me. It was instinctual for me when growing up, and it still feels right today. I even allow my horses to say "no" sometimes instead of always dictating what they should do.

Have you ever heard of such heresy?!

The truth is, when you allow your horse to do this, he will thank you for it. And you will suddenly see a noticeable change in his responses and demeanor as the light sparkles in his eyes.

This unique blend of insight, understanding, and empathy has provided me with the tools to create a truly flexible approach, which can easily be modified and adjusted to any situation and any horse.

We are all individuals and so are our horses, and when you take the leap to allow your horse to have his say in your relationship, the connection, communication, and companionship you've always dreamt of become possible.

My burning desire is to help both humans and their horses get to know each other better. By doing this they can become the best possible partners for each other and guarantee that the horse gets the forever-loving home he deserves.

Many people, especially women, naturally resonate with this

softer, more sympathetic approach. As an example, one student recently wrote to me:

"Since I have been following your courses and learning to 'listen to my horse', we have had some lovely moments of connection that I would never have had if I had stayed on my path of go, go, go. Grab my horse, groom and out for a ride. These days my rides are much more leisurely. Thank you for all your insight, Teddie."

I've had the privilege and pleasure of helping thousands of students reach success over the past three decades and I have personally worked with over five hundred horses, so you can rest assured what you are about to learn has been thoroughly road-tested.

Case Study #1: Pamela and Cody

Pamela first came to me as many of my students do:

- Frustrated
- Confused
- Not knowing where to turn to find answers

Like many of my clients, Pamela wasn't new to horses. She had owned horses for years and had a few different types of horses. Pamela knew the basics and was pretty confident in her horsemanship abilities. She knew there was more out there to learn, but she was happy with what she knew as it was working for her and her horses.

She had rescued a mare named Asha whom she loved dearly. Asha was already trained to ride and was a good horse. They got along well and her current knowledge was all she needed to make things work with Asha and everything was going well. Then she decided she had enough room at her home to also rescue Asha's son, Cody.

That's when the trouble started.

Cody had not been trained to ride nor was he as consistent a horse as Asha was. Pamela tried everything she knew to train Cody but one day while doing the basic groundwork she realized that he had terrible anxiety.

She wasn't sure what triggered it but because of this anxiety Cody wasn't happy being haltered, and would rear, buck, pull back and even chew on the lead rope. Sometimes he would bolt or even worse, get aggressive and charge her as well as being constantly pushy and nippy. He was definitely a handful.

Cody's anxieties were high and this brought up anxieties in Pamela and she felt her growing fear of failure was also beginning to get in the way.

The good part was that Cody clearly wanted a close relationship with Pamela. But Pamela didn't know how to have that relationship without him getting pushy and nippy or worse. He would allow her to do some things like picking up and rasping his hooves and he would back away from her when she asked him to, even with his food dish in her hands.

When she would just sit with him in the pasture, she could tell that he wanted to be close to her. But what was strange was that Cody didn't want her brushing or petting him most of the time and he would threaten to bite her when she tried. This just added to her confusion about how to handle him. He wasn't acting like any other horse she had ever had.

And as much as she wanted to try to start him under saddle, she knew that she had to get to a better place in their relationship on the ground first and that if she didn't, the possibility of her being thrown off or hurt would be high. She wanted to be safe and didn't get this feeling while around Cody.

She wanted to do it right the first time and be as safe as possible so she joined my **Personal Coaching Program (PCP)** and we went to work by first doing what I call *"hitting the reset button."*

Within two weeks she noticed a difference in how Cody was reacting to her. He was softening and listening. Each week he showed more and more improvement. Pamela couldn't believe how quickly Cody's personality went from aggressive to loving.

After six months the magic happened and Cody became the horse she knew was there deep down. The anxiety subsided and the two of them started working together as a real team.

Pamela told me, *"I finally found the KEY to Cody"*. Now she can pet him anywhere, anytime. He no longer attacks or bites. He's gentle and thinks about their interactions, is willing to listen to her, and is so sweet. She says that Cody is soft and lovely to be with now. Most importantly though, Pamela now feels safe around Cody.

He is also much better on a halter and is no longer high-energy, pushy and aggressive, and he stays right with her no matter where they go around the farm. He even takes direction from her without issue now because he wants to please her. He enjoys her company.

Cody is much more respectful around food as well. They are a family of three and everyone is calm and happy, a totally different dynamic to the way it was before. Pamela feels like she has been accepted as a part of the herd and they all do things together as a family.

It is a totally different relationship with Cody now too. He is a lot more patient and will wait at the gate while she opens it so they go through together as a team. Then he waits for her to turn around with him and close the gate before they go to the front to eat some grass. He used to push, run through, and be highly anxious and sometimes dangerous when going through the gate. Now the whole process is smooth and easy.

She has learned to relax and has learned how to calm Cody down as well. Pamela is much more confident with no more fear of failure. And while he may still try to take charge sometimes, Pamela knows how to handle it safely and effectively now, so that he quickly gets back to being relaxed and cooperative.

After she got the horse she truly wanted and could work with, we started working on training Cody to be ridden. After a year of working together and starting over from scratch, Cody is not only a different horse, but he is just about ready to be backed and ridden without issue.

So you see, with the right frame of mind, patience, love, and the right guidance... magic can happen. You can get the results you want and very quickly. You don't have to spend years and years trying to figure it out on your own, you can get to the results you want quicker than you thought possible.

It's incredible the kind of impact and transformation you can have with your horse when you use this approach. If you're open-minded and willing to get out of your comfort zone to try new things, this approach will work for anyone and any horse.

Case Study #2: Madeleine and Choupette

Madeleine's story is an inspiring one for those looking to make a radical shift beyond just a few issues.

Madeleine, again like so many of my clients, is not new to horses. She has been a horse enthusiast for a long time and has owned a few different horses during that time. She is also an avid learner and has taken lessons and gone to clinics with some very well-known trainers (you'd recognize their names).

Madeleine had had an amazing connection with her previous horse, an Andalusian called Bravada, and got as far as riding her bitless.

Sadly though, Bravada passed away and so Madeleine set out on the hunt for a new horse to have in her life.

Fast forward a few years and she fell in love with a beautiful Haflinger mare named Choupette. Choupette was 7 years old and as she had been at a riding school, Madeleine assumed that she would be well-trained.

However, Choupette had been returned to the school four months previously because she had no forward movement. Madeleine thought, *"No problem, I can handle that,"* so she purchased the little Haflinger and brought her home.

One and a half years later, not only did Choupette still have no forward movement but Madeleine discovered that she had a lot of other vices too.

She was very pushy and would squeeze Madeleine between fences, box walls, gates, whatever was handy. She would rear up when she was just being walked on a lead into her pasture. She balked when Madeleine tried to insist she move forward. Then she would rear and sometimes charge her when asked to move.

Even when Madeleine asked Choupette to lunge, she reared up and charged her. She also kicked Madeleine the first time she brought her food and would run her over in the pasture without warning. In short, Choupette was a dangerous horse to be around.

When Madeleine tried to ride Choupette, it was only at a

walk and only where and when Choupette wanted. This was definitely a one-sided relationship, and not in favor of the human!

Madeleine did all she knew to fix the issues. She did groundwork, clicker training, and everything else she had learned, but nothing seemed to work. When she asked Choupette for a trot or a canter while riding, Choupette would shake her head and go directly to the mounting block and stand there, basically saying, *"Get off my back"*.

Choupette wasn't afraid of anything either and was desensitized to everything: flags, whips, noises, even jumping up and down screaming, nothing moved her. Choupette was also extremely stubborn and wasn't going to do anything she didn't want to do. And if Madeleine tried to force the issue, she would get aggressive and dangerous without any regard for who was close by.

Add onto that food aggressive, pushy, nippy, anxious, nervous, not wanting to go into the barn, pulling, bolting, getting out of the stall or pasture and escaping, and almost every other horse-related issue you can think of.

Now, let me be totally frank here...

I wasn't sure I could help her, especially as we were doing all this over the phone during the pandemic. A horse with so many issues that couldn't even be fixed by an experienced horse person that truly loved this horse. This was going to be a tough one.

But Madeleine kept repeating, *"I love her and want what is best for her"*. I could hear the pain in her voice, love mixed with absolute end of the line frustration. She told me that if I couldn't help her that she would have to sell Choupette.

I could feel the deep sadness in her heart and it broke mine too. How could I not try? I had to help her.

So, she started my **Personal Coaching Program (PCP)** by going back to the basics. Madeleine had an open mind and was a great student. She was very enthusiastic to learn how my fundamentals of horsemanship were different. And she was even more surprised how my fine-tuning, tweaks, and the small details made such a big difference. Within a very short time, Choupette began to transform.

Madeleine then moved on from the basics to all the games and exercises in my program and Choupette started having fun as her playful nature came out. She was now interested in what Madeleine was doing. She wanted to go out and play and do the exercises. She not only started listening to Madeleine, but she was completely focused. This was new and exciting. Choupette now had a pep in her step and was trotting on cue and enjoying every minute they spent together.

Plus, when Choupette had a bad day now and again, like we all do, Madeleine became confident in how to handle it. Life with Choupette was now a give and take on both sides. One day Madeleine did what Choupette wanted and the next day Choupette would gladly do whatever Madeleine wanted. It was a true partnership and they were fast becoming best friends.

Six months later and Madeleine had the horse she had always dreamt Choupette could be.

But we didn't stop there. I knew there was more the two of them could achieve so we kept going. Six months after that, Madeleine was ecstatic with how well the two of them got along and the depth of their relationship.

Now they go out on rides together at a trot and even canter playfully on trails. Madeleine even rides her bitless. She says that she can see and feel how happy Choupette is. The difference in Choupette's behavior is night and day.

She has never seen her so playful. Choupette, runs around, playfully bucking and rearing and canters over to greet Madeleine when she goes out to see her. Choupette is so considerate now that when Madeleine gets there, Choupette calms down right away and is very respectful of Madeleine's space.

Choupette is now a totally different horse, very well-mannered, happy, and safe to be around on the ground and in the saddle.

Case Study #3: Melissa and Barnie

Melissa came to me in the same way a lot of students do; curious, searching for something she was missing with her horse.

Many times they can't really pinpoint it down to a specific 'thing' they are missing, it's more of a feeling. They can feel the large gap between what they have and what they want with their horse.

And the issue isn't only that there is a gap they can feel, but they also can't figure out how to bridge that gap. It's not that they haven't tried either. Most of my clients, like Melissa, have had a horse before and have pretty good horsemanship skills. So by the time they come to me they have tried for months, if not years, to both fill the gap and fix the issues they are having with their horse.

I always hear that "this horse is different". There's something about the horse they have now that isn't working like it did with other horses they've had. And because something is different, the training or fixes that they are trying aren't working either. So, they try and try again with little or no success. Many times they just give up and settle for what they have and let go of their dreams.

However, Melissa wasn't about to give up. But after trying and trying many times she was honest enough to admit she needed help. That's when she called me, we talked things through, and she decided to join my **Personal Coaching Program (PCP)**.

The main issue was that her horse Barnie was very anxious

and nervous and Melissa didn't have the confidence to handle him and bring him through by herself. He was very spooky and reared up on her a few times while riding and it really scared her.

Melissa also said that she and Barnie didn't really have a connection. She had a good connection with her other horse Gracie, but she didn't know how to get the same thing with Barnie. Melissa had tried to figure it out on her own, but it just wasn't working with Barnie like it did with Gracie.

Barnie was also high strung and hard to manage when walking on a lead out of the pasture. And when something spooked him, he would act up or run. When he saw a saddle coming out, his eyes would get big and his nostrils would flare.

As a result of all this, Barnie didn't trust Melissa and she didn't trust him.

Plus, Barnie was afraid of going through certain areas in his pasture and he was food aggressive, pushy, didn't listen when asked to move away, was constantly bossy, and sometimes he would simply ignore her.

However, the first time she saw a picture of Barnie, Melissa knew that he was the one for her. It was love at first sight. She wanted to do right by Barnie and do whatever she could to help him be as safe and happy as possible.

Melissa's horsemanship skills worked fine with Gracie, but for some reason they weren't working the same way with Barnie. The approach I teach in my coaching program was just what she needed to get the trust, connection, and willingness she wanted with Barnie. All within an online program that she could do at her own pace with access to me personally whenever she wanted.

- Within the first month Barnie became calmer and more attentive and started to soften, which came as an unexpected surprise for Melissa.
- By month three, Barnie was a different horse. Practically all his issues had dissolved and he and Melissa were able to start relaxing into their relationship together.
- Month six now and the trust between them has been well and truly established. He listens to her, is calm and attentive, walks and trots right beside her, and is really good. More than that though, Barnie is far happier, more expressive and wonderfully playful. He is excited about being with Melissa and pays lots of attention to her. The best part is that they have a much stronger connection and a much better relationship.

They are now in the part of the program where we are working on groundwork for riding, which is also going very well. When something spooks him, Barnie is now able to remain calm and wait for Melissa's instruction.

Melissa says that it's so wonderful now because they handle whatever situation comes up together as a team. She is really confident in Barnie and he in her because they understand each other so much better. She has learned to read his body language and his eyes, and she knows what he's thinking and feeling at any given moment.

For Melissa, having exactly what she wants with her horse has been a game-changer. She's happy and Barnie is happy. She's confident in her newfound horsemanship skills and her ability to work with Barnie under any circumstances.

If you're here looking for ways to bridge that gap you're feeling, or to find what you feel you're missing, you'll want to focus on the chapters in this book where I talk about options and choices.

By learning to look at the world from your horse's perspective, you will not only create a new dynamic between you but at the same time a deeper love, a deeper understanding, and a deeper relationship than you've ever imagined. The transformation will be magical for both you and your horse.

Gain the horse of your dreams and give your horse the person of his dreams. This is what is possible and what awaits you.

CHAPTER
ONE

Herd-Bound Behaviors

"Conflict cannot survive without your participation."
WAYNE DYER

I have had horses in the past who were herd-bound at one point or another. Most of the time it took me a very short amount of time to fix this behavior. So I didn't pay too much attention or put too much emphasis on teaching others how to fix this problem unless they asked about it. But I have since learned that this is a much more common issue than I had previously thought.

When it has occurred, there are a few approaches I have turned to that have always worked for me. Resolving an issue early on is like treating a serious illness as early as possible. It stops any major problems early and can be corrected simpler and quicker than if left untreated. At least that was my thinking, until recently.

No matter how long you have horses, the one thing you learn is that you never know everything. There is always more to know and updated information to learn. My horses continue to teach me new lessons to this very day and I know I will be learning from horses for the rest of my life.

My recent lesson was that there is such a thing as the perfect storm when it comes to horses and herd-bound behavior. And the horse that became the poster-child for this perfect storm was my very own Apollo.

This meant that my simple, tried-and-true solutions were not going to work when faced with a full-blown emotional meltdown. I had never had a horse before that became herd-bound so quickly and so severely.

Here is the story behind my worst-case, herd-bound scenario with Apollo and the reason why I decided to write this book, because I don't want you to have to go through the same trauma.

You'd think that with a horse I've had for thirty years all the possible problems would have been ironed out. Well, that's certainly what I thought as Apollo was usually sweet, reliable and fun-loving. But that turned out not to be the case.

Here's what happened...

We had moved to a new facility and Apollo became so deeply connected to his new pasture buddy, Harry, that he became severely herd-bound. He ran around like a nutcase every time Harry's owner took Harry out to ride. And I do mean nutcase. Apollo would run as hard as he could with no regard as to where he was going or what was around him.

He became severely herd-bound very quickly, which was a total surprise to me. It wasn't like he had become mildly herd-bound and then slowly ramped up. Nope, he went from 0–100 on the herd-bound-o-meter in a heartbeat.

But after really thinking about it, I could understand why. He had lost his father, Jazz, and his best friend, D'Artagnan, within months of each other. And then he'd lost his home, where he had lived for four years, and his six horse friends who shared a fence line with him a few months after that. The poor guy was sad, lonely, and scared. He went from a herd of nine horses to being one single horse in a new facility.

This was a horrible situation that I could not avoid. The boarding facility where he was living was sold, and all the horses had to leave within sixty days. All the owners tried to move to the same facility so our horses would be close again, but that didn't work out.

When Apollo first moved into his new home and pasture, his new pasture mate, Harry, had an abscess. So Harry wasn't taken out of the pasture much, and the two of them took care of each other and bonded hard and fast.

They were the only two horses in this large pasture. They shared one fence line with two mares who normally stayed on the opposite side of their pasture. Another fence line was facing a large pasture with only one horse and the other two fence lines were facing a dense forest. So the only company Apollo had was Harry.

Then to top that off, there were wild animals that came into the pastures like deer, racoons, beavers, and vultures. Plus a freight train that ran past the farm four times a day. It was far enough away that the horses didn't see it, but close enough to make a lot of noise as it went past. And because there was a crossing to get into the farm, the train would blow its horn every time it passed. This was all new to Apollo.

Here's how the Herd-Bound Issue began...

Unfortunately for Apollo, once Harry was healthy again, his owner took him out almost daily to ride. When he left the pasture Apollo would walk around looking for him off and on. Nothing really out of the ordinary. He would walk along the fence line and then quickly settle down and start eating grass.

Ray, a large Belgian horse, was in the pasture across the driveway from Apollo and they would keep each other company when Harry left. Ray's pasture was the closest to Apollo, but they didn't share a fence line, and Ray wasn't always in sight. So having Ray around to keep Apollo company only worked if Ray was in sight.

At first I thought, *"No big deal. Apollo will be fine and everything will work out."* But for some reason, Apollo actually got much worse, very quickly. Every time Harry left, Apollo would now run along the fence line and run the entire length of the pasture as hard as he could. He galloped down the pasture, stopped, whinnied, turned around and then would run back to the other side of the pasture and do it all over again.

The behavior changed practically overnight. He was fine and then all of a sudden he wasn't fine. I tried to go into the pasture when Apollo was doing this to calm him down, but he didn't even care that I was there. He was only focused on one thing: Harry.

Harry was gone, and Apollo desperately wanted to be with him. He did not listen or pay any attention to me, and he wouldn't let me catch him. He was so distracted that I knew I had to be careful because if I got too close, he would run me over without a second thought.

Apollo had gone from being my sweet, well-behaved, baby boy to being a very dangerous horse to be around. Because of this, I knew my easy solutions were not going to work with him because of the severity of the case.

Let me give you a general overview of my worst-case scenario fix. In a later chapter I will go into the details of how to resolve a severe case with your horse which you can follow step-by-step.

When it gets as bad as it was with Apollo, the main issue to deal with is:

How do you stop your horse from hurting himself without hurting yourself in the process?

This is the three-part process I used with Apollo:

- Step #1 – Take Apollo out on his own without Harry, leaving Harry in the pasture, and keep Apollo calm and happy.
- Step #2 – Take Apollo and Harry out of the pasture at the same time and have them do things separately.
- Step #3 – Take Harry out of the pasture and stay with Apollo in the pasture, keeping him calm and happy

Step #1

Once I was able to calm Apollo down enough to safely get a halter on him (the preliminary process), I started this three-part process. The first step was taking Apollo out daily and leaving Harry in the pasture by himself. That worked great. Apollo was happy to leave Harry, and he loved going for walks with me. He stayed calm and happy without any real issues of being herd-bound.

This was helping, but Apollo would still run around like a crazy horse whenever Harry left the pasture. He was so focused on Harry that he didn't care about his own welfare and I was a bit worried he would slip and hurt himself when it was muddy from the rain or snow. There wasn't much I could do though. So I just had to cross my fingers and hope and pray that he didn't get seriously hurt when Harry left the pasture as I wasn't there to calm him down every second of every day.

Step #2

I took Apollo out for a walk at the same time Harry's owner took him for a ride. This worked great too. Apollo had no issues getting out and going for a walk with me even though Harry was going in the opposite direction. He showed mild signs of herd-bound behavior and was a bit anxious and looked around for Harry. But it was nothing that I couldn't fix, so I worked on those issues as and when needed.

I didn't ride Apollo when we went for a walk because I couldn't trust him not to flip out like he did in the pasture. I didn't want to risk being thrown off so he could go find Harry. So we went for a walk along the trails side by side with a halter and lead. This way if anything went wrong, I could just let Apollo go, and I wouldn't get pulled, thrown off, or dragged.

I had not gotten to Step #3 yet when unfortunately Apollo did hurt himself. It was winter and the first day that the ground had frozen solid Apollo injured his stifle by galloping down the pasture, stopping and turning around too quickly on the frozen hard ground and slipping. Poor guy.

The vet came out and said, *"It's not too bad, and it should only take about six to eight weeks to heal completely. He doesn't need stall rest, but you should keep him from running around too much."*

My first thought was, *"How in the heck am I going to do that?"* Especially with Harry going out for a ride almost every day, regardless of the weather. Seriously? Now this whole process had just gotten a lot more complicated.

I spoke with Harry's owner, explained the situation, and asked her if she could allow Harry to stay with Apollo for at least one week without her going out for a ride. That would allow Apollo the time to rest that he needed to at least start his recovery. She said, *"No"*. I was shocked. She was going to continue doing what she had always done without regard for how it affected anyone else.

Now what?

I was determined to find a solution that was good for Apollo. Because if she kept taking Harry out every day and Apollo continued to run around on his injured leg, it would get much worse very quickly. Plus, I don't live that close to the facility and Harry's owner didn't always come at the same time each day, so I couldn't just pop down there to stop Apollo running on his bad leg.

I thought about it all night and worried.

- I couldn't put him in a stall by himself because it would cause too much anxiety and stress, which could bring on colic.
- I couldn't leave him out there alone when Harry went off to ride because he would run around and cause more damage to his injury.
- We couldn't move Harry out and a new horse in because Apollo would still be running around trying to find Harry. It would even be worse, as it would be a lot longer than just during a ride.
- I couldn't put him in with Ray because Ray's owner said he had to be alone because he didn't like other horses and would attack.

Despite all these hurdles, I was determined to make lemonade out of these lemons!

So I asked Harry's owner to let me know when she was going out to the barn to ride. That way, I could be out there to keep Apollo calm while she was gone and he wouldn't hurt himself even worse.

Thankfully she said okay to that, even though that meant I had to stop whatever I was doing and leave my house whenever Harry's owner texted me. But I was willing to do that for Apollo's sake. No matter what day, or time of day, or type of weather, I would drop everything just to make sure Apollo was safe.

That's what a good horse mom does, right?

Apollo's injury pushed me to go to Step #3 quicker than I would have liked but I didn't have much choice.

Step #3

This is where I was going to keep Apollo calm and happy in the pasture while Harry left the pasture.

The first day I did this, Apollo became a horse I had never seen before - wild and crazy! He became that dangerous horse I talked about earlier. And this is why communication is so important in cases like this, when you are trying to work around someone else's schedule.

Harry's owner had texted me that she would be at the farm in an hour but despite managing to get there in thirty minutes, she had already taken Harry out of the pasture and was out of sight. So much for her giving me notice!

By the time I got there Apollo was running up and down the fence line on three legs and kind of hopping on the other. He was upset, high-strung, had started to sweat, and wouldn't stop moving and whinnying. Plus, he was in pain.

This lapse in Harry's owner's judgment took us back to square one and actually made Apollo's injury much worse.

So as a general request, please always try to think about how what you're doing might affect another horse or a person near the horse. Thank you.

Apollo was so upset that when I went in to halter him, I couldn't catch him. He wouldn't listen to me at all. He was so frantic that he actually ran through the metal fencing, ripping it apart, and catching his bad leg on the fence. At least this gave me a few minutes to quickly halter him and get him unstuck. Luckily, he didn't do any more damage to himself. He knew he was in trouble when he got stuck and he trusted me enough to stop and let me help him. Otherwise it could have been so much worse.

After I haltered him, I took him into the run-in shed to check him out for cuts and to give him some treats and calm him down. But it was a bit too late for that, the panic had already set in and Apollo wouldn't stop moving. He kept whinnying and pushing into me, and he even kicked out at me with his injured leg. He was very dangerous and unruly. The only thing I could do now was to keep him from running around and hurting himself more and to stay out of his kick zone.

He was in panic mode, and I was in emergency mode. Luckily, Harry came back after about an hour and Apollo had settled down enough for me to touch him and check him out. But for the first hour he was limping, wouldn't stop moving, was frantic and freaked out and I couldn't get close. It was almost as if he was afraid that something bad was going to happen to Harry and he had to get to him to save him. He was that focused on getting out to Harry.

Once Harry was back in the pasture, all was fine, and it was as if nothing had ever happened. But I did notice that Harry was now limping. Something had happened to him on the ride. Which was why I think Apollo was extra nervous about this particular time away from Harry. It turns out Harry had slipped on the ice while cantering down the driveway, which was covered with compacted snow and icy patches. Why his owner decided to canter him there is anyone's guess.

At least Apollo calmed down and became quiet again with Harry back in the pasture. He stood still and grazed as if everything was normal - even though I felt like I was on the brink of having a heart attack!

Before Harry's owner took off, I stressed to her how important it was for Apollo's health that Harry not be taken out without me being there. She wasn't happy about it, but reluctantly, she agreed to help.

On the second day Harry's owner gave me a time to get to the farm, I got there about twenty minutes early. And guess what? I found her taking Harry out of the pasture and getting ready to leave again. I couldn't believe it. If I had gotten there on time, we would have been in the same situation as the day before.

But, luckily, I was able to grab the halter and fetch Apollo before he went ballistic again. She couldn't have cared less how her actions had caused more pain and injury to my horse or that her horse was still limping. And she wasn't listening to anything I had to say.

What was interesting though on this day was that Apollo only whinnied a few times as Harry left, and only paced back and forth a few times. It was as if he was saying, *"Hey, I don't know what your problem is, but I don't care if Harry leaves."* He was a different horse than the day before, and I had to figure out why so I could get this result next time.

Even though Apollo was pretty calm, let me groom and pet him, and enjoyed some quality belly scratches, he wouldn't eat anything while Harry was gone. When Harry came back two hours later, Apollo acted like he hadn't even missed him.

It was encouraging to see the change from the day before and even from earlier that day, so I continued doing Step #3 for a few weeks until Apollo's stifle injury was healed and he was no longer herd-bound to Harry. Luckily, they both happened at the same time, and it only took an additional three weeks.

I have always believed that everything happens for a reason, and I was determined to find a silver lining in this mess. My silver lining was that I got to spend some amazing, quality time with Apollo. It gave us both the chance to bond and get better connected at this new facility.

Apollo lost his herd-bound behavior and was now happy to be in his new surroundings. He was now happy to be with me over being with Harry and he preferred my company again over that of other horses. He was my sweet angel again.

So that's the long and short of why fixing herd-bound behavior is so important. That's also why I decided to write this short book to help others who are going through the same issues I was.

Before we continue, here are...

2 important questions to ask yourself

The next two questions that I want you to answer before we get into the step-by-step solutions are...

1. Do I need to resolve this issue?
2. Why do I need to resolve this issue?

If your answer to Question #1 is something like, *"Because my friend told me I need to control my horse,"* which means that you don't see a problem, then your answer is "No". You do not need to resolve this issue if it is not causing you problems. If you don't have any issues with your horse's behavior and it's not causing him or you any problems, then again, the answer is "No". You do not need to resolve this issue.

If your answer to Question #2 is something like, *"Because my friend told me that this is bad behavior that I need to correct but I'm not sure why,"* then the answer is, *"I don't."* If you don't know why you need to resolve this issue, or you don't feel the need to resolve this issue, then again, you don't need to do anything about it.

I know that sounds counterproductive but I don't want you doing something because someone else told you that you need to, especially if it isn't causing you or your horse any problems. If it is causing issues, then that's different.

Let me give you an example.

At one point in my life, I only had two horses, Jazz and his son Apollo. The three of us did everything together. We would go on rides together. I would ride Jazz and pony Apollo, and we had a great time. I never needed to, nor did I want to, ride only one horse without taking the other with me.

I lived alone and lived near a national park with riding trails that spanned a few hundred acres. These were public riding trails through a nature preserve. But I hardly ever saw anyone else out on these trails. It was usually just the three of us and all the nature we could handle. In my eyes, it was something we did together as a herd, and it was a blessing. Why not share it with both horses at the same time if there weren't any issues in doing so?

We also worked and trained together. I would let them both out in the arena together to play. Then the three of us would work on different lessons, either one-to-one or both of them together. It all depended on the lesson.

Then one day, someone asked me if my horses were herd-bound and if that was why I took both of them riding together. At the time, I didn't know much about horses being herd-bound, plus I didn't have any issues. My horses didn't show any of the signs and symptoms I described earlier.

She couldn't relate to the idea of working with more than one horse at a time. Her belief system told her that I was only supposed to work with one horse at a time. Me working with two horses at the same time was alien to her.

No one had ever taught me or told me that I should only work with one horse at a time. So it was not a belief system that I adhered to. It's amazing the things you can do when no one tells you that you can't. She kept asking me why I took both horses with me when I went out on trails. My only answer was (1) because I loved it and enjoyed it and (2) because "I CAN."

The point of this story is that if you don't have an issue with your horses being together all the time and it is not causing any problems, then you don't need to worry about your horses being herd-bound. If they are, they are, and if it's okay, then it's okay.

In other words, don't worry about what someone else says you should or shouldn't do, especially when it's just based on their map of the world and their personal belief system, not yours.

How to Resolve a Mild Case of Herd-Bound Behavior

"You cannot always control what goes on outside.
But you can always control what goes on inside."
WAYNE DYER

My process for horses where only one is mildly herd-bound – (Timeframe: 2–3 weeks)

This is the process I've used to remove mild herd-bound behavior in one horse. It allowed me to take that same horse out of the pasture for walks and rides without any of the herd-bound behavioral issues.

Here is my mild case story:

For years I have had my two horses at boarding facilities where they were in separate paddocks that shared a fence line.

Sometimes, I was able to put them both in one large pasture together and as they are father and son, they have always done very well together. Sometimes there has been the occasional issue over food when housed in the same pasture but otherwise it was always very harmonious.

Even though it's always been the two of them as a family for years, I never had to deal with them being herd-bound. Part of that was because they were in boarding facilities and had other horses around. So when I took one or the other out to ride, occasionally, they had other friends. As I mentioned in the last chapter, many times I took them out together, riding one and ponying the other. We had a lot of fun together.

Then I found a great little place where I could live with my horses on a five-acre property. I was thrilled. I thought my horses would be, too, since I could see them every day and we would have a lot more time together. I'm sure they loved seeing me every day and doing a lot more together. But I also think they missed having a lot of other horses around.

We had been at our new home for about a month before I took Jazz out to check out the trails. I wanted to make sure everyone was settled in and felt comfortable before exploring the property. Jazz was great. We walked side by side along all the trails and were out exploring together for about an hour. When we came back, Apollo was eating grass and whinnied a hello and then went back to eating again. No issues from either horse.

The next day I decided it was Apollo's turn to go exploring with me. So we haltered up and started out on the trails. We had only been out for about five minutes when I heard Jazz calling to Apollo. That was a first. That was not Jazz's normal behavior. He had always been fine when I took Apollo out before, just like Apollo had been fine the day before when I took Jazz out.

Not today. We went a bit further, and Jazz called to Apollo again. Apollo didn't seem to care and didn't even whinny back. That worried Jazz more, and I heard Jazz running around the paddock. And to clarify, Jazz didn't whinny to Apollo until we were out of sight.

So I started back, and as I turned around, Apollo whinnied back to Jazz. I think he realized Jazz was worried, and he wanted to reassure him he was okay. Once we got back to the trail opening where Jazz could see Apollo again, he calmed down and started grazing. I then took Apollo into the arena and played with him there, and Jazz didn't seem to care, presumably because he could see Apollo the whole time.

Even though Jazz had been on those trails the day before without showing any signs of spookiness, he was now upset with Apollo going on them. I'm not sure why. But something was different, and I needed to make them feel comfortable again. I'm pretty sure it was the fact that their herd was now just the two of them and they needed to watch out for each other more. They couldn't count on other horses doing that as they did at the boarding facilities.

So the next day, I took Jazz out and went on the same trails, and he was happy and excited to be going out. He had pep in his step and was walking a bit faster than I was. He couldn't wait to go exploring again. And Apollo, who was left in the paddock, was fine. No crying out, no running around, no worried looks, nothing. He was happily grazing when we got back. So it was obvious that Jazz was the only one showing mild herd-bound behaviors when he was left in the pasture. But he had no issues when Apollo was left in the pasture and he was the one taken out.

I thought maybe Jazz was jealous that Apollo was going out

without him and that I was paying more attention to him. The next day I tried taking Apollo out again without Jazz, and sure enough, he did the same thing, but a little worse. Jazz started running along the fence line, whinnying and acting up.

As mentioned earlier, I like to 'Push the Easy Button' whenever possible, so I started with the easiest solution to this problem to see if it worked before I started on a more complicated solution.

I thought that if Jazz had something to occupy his mind and tummy when I left that he wouldn't mind Apollo leaving. So I gave him a bucket full of special treats to eat while we were gone. But he didn't seem to care about the special treats and didn't touch them once I took Apollo out of the pasture. When we were back in sight though, he set about eating the treats.

We did this a few days in a row and Jazz started to realize that when Apollo left, he got treats like carrots, apples, and alfalfa. I would put the treats down and let Jazz start eating and get comfortable while I haltered Apollo. Then once he was calm, I would take Apollo out of the pasture.

The more I did this, the more Jazz calmed down, but the issue wasn't 100 percent fixed because as soon as we were out of sight, Jazz started running around and whinnying again. That meant that I had half of the fix but needed to find the other half.

Note: If Jazz acted up too much when I left with Apollo, I would stop where we were and just graze. This way Jazz could see Apollo and he would calm down. Then if he acted up too much again when Apollo and I started to go further away, I would take Apollo back into the pasture and pick up the treats that I had left for Jazz. Apollo in the pasture equaled no treats. Apollo out of the pasture equaled lots of treats. This worked since Jazz really enjoyed his treats.

The behavior was a mild type of herd-bound behavior. It may have started because Jazz was used to having other horses around, plus perhaps a little jealousy that it was me and Apollo going out together.

The other half of the easy solution I came up with was to take both Jazz and Apollo out on the trails together. That way they could explore together, learn that the trails were safe and that they didn't need the other to protect them. That was my job, and this helped reassure them that I would do my job and protect them on these new trails. It also bonded the three of us even closer as a herd. I wanted both of my horses to trust me to protect them on the trails.

I did this for over a week. Then one day Jazz decided he didn't want to go out with us. So I left him in the paddock with a bunch of alfalfa hay that I had just put down and he was absolutely fine from then on.

So that was all it took. I could now take each of them out on trails where they couldn't see each other. They both were sure that the other one would come back, and they were both confident that I would keep them safe. You could see the calmness and confidence in Jazz now as we left. Jazz had developed a trust in me to protect Apollo when we were gone and knew that I would bring Apollo back to him safely.

Occasionally, when I was riding one or the other on those trails, they would whinny to each other. But that was it, and it was only once to say, *"Hey, you okay?"* and the other would whinny back, *"Everything is good."*

I made sure I maintained that camaraderie between the three of us by taking them both out and walking the trails or the farm together, happily exploring as a herd. This became a weekly occurrence that we all looked forward to.

I think sometimes Jazz was actually happy to see me leave and go riding with Apollo, because when I left, he got to eat the good stuff. I would always leave him a bucket full of special treats or a few flakes of Alfalfa just to say thank you for being so good when we went on trails. The combination of having special food when Apollo left, plus the trust and bonding we did, dissipated all the herd-bound behaviors Jazz had.

Luckily, that was the extent of the herd-bound behavior. It only took me a week to figure out what was going on and another week to fix it. Then a few months later I got another horse, D'Artagnan, and Jazz never had an issue again. Even though Jazz preferred my company over that of Apollo, he was glad to have a friend when Apollo left the pasture.

I've successfully used this approach to help my students correct their mild cases as well. It worked every time. Hopefully, your horse's herd-bound behaviors are as easy to fix and this story helps you with a solution. Remember to *Push the Easy Button*' whenever possible.

CHAPTER
THREE

How to Resolve a Medium Case of Herd-Bound Behavior

"Open your mind to all possibilities, because
whether you believe something is possible or
impossible, either way you'll be right."
WAYNE DYER

M y process for horses where only one has a medium case of herd-bound behavior – (Timeframe: 3–4 weeks)

This is the process I've used to remove medium herd-bound behavior in one horse. Once finished, it allowed me to take out that horse for walks and rides alone without any herd-bound behavioral issues so it became a pleasure instead of a hassle.

<u>Here is my medium case story:</u>

After the mild case of herd-bound behavior with Jazz was

resolved, I could ride each of my horses alone on trails. Even after I purchased a new horse, D'Artagnan, I could still ride out on Jazz or Apollo without any herd-bound issues. The three of us were working well together as a herd - Jazz, his son Apollo, and my new horse D'Artagnan. At this point, Jazz was twenty-eight and had been with me for twenty-seven years, and his son Apollo was twenty-four and had been with me all his life.

D'Artagnan was a beautiful four-year-old black Andalusian wild stallion. When I first purchased him, I kept the three of them separated so they could get to know each other and get acquainted slowly. I wasn't sure I would be able to socialize a stallion with two geldings, but that was my plan.

Luckily it worked out fine and they only had a few initial disagreements before settling down in a large pasture as a happy herd of three, plus me.

D'Artagnan was the young, strong, dominant horse. Jazz was the older lead horse, and Apollo was the shy, submissive horse. They all had their place in the herd, and it went smoothly. None of them cared who went out with me to ride because there were always two left in the pasture.

During the spring, I started to ride Jazz more, as he was my preferred trail horse. We could go out for hours together exploring. During this time Apollo and D'Artagnan became closer and became real buddies. Even when all three were in the pasture, you could see Apollo and D'Artagnan teaming up together more often, and poor Jazz would be grazing close by, but alone. Not always, but often enough to notice the change. Before that, it had been Jazz and Apollo teaming up with D'Artagnan on his own.

Jazz didn't seem to mind as he got lots of time with me. Jazz and D'Artagnan were never really close and there always seemed to be a bit of jealousy between them as to who got more of my attention.

Then one day I decided to take Apollo out for some quality time with me on the trails. Jazz just went on his merry way and went to grazing. But D'Artagnan now got all upset that Apollo was leaving the pasture. This was new.

He started running up and down the fence line, whinnying, kicking up, and acting like I was taking his best friend away forever. So I started doing the same procedure as in Chapter 2 to treat a mild case of herd-bound behavior. But D'Artagnan wanted to be with Apollo, not me. So even when I took D'Artagnan out to go for a walk and do things with me and left Apollo in the pasture, he still acted up.

Okay, he didn't want Apollo to leave him, and he didn't want to leave Apollo. Now what? This was now a bit more complex than just a mild case. D'Artagnan was now my medium case of herd-bound behavior. So if your horse isn't a mild case and needs a bit more to help resolve the herd-bound issues, then here is another solution for you that worked with D'Artagnan.

Read through the entire process first so you can map out a good time to do the whole process. This way you aren't stopping and starting, which will slow the process and hurt the results.

Step I - Hit the Reset Button – 1 week (4–6 times a week)

The first thing we are going to do to set the scene is hit the reset button for both you and your horse. This may feel like you're watching grass grow, but this really is the most important part of resolving the herd-bound behavior. It will give you the same bonding experience that Jazz, Apollo, and I had when we went on trails together in the mild case. You need this bonding to develop more trust in and from your horse.

Note: I want you to commit to going out to your horses for the next six days (out of seven). You can skip one day during the week, but only one to make this part effective. If not, you can take two weeks to do this by going out to your horse at least three times a week.

For the first week:

I want you to go into the pasture with both of your horses and just hang out for 30–45 minutes each time.

That means take a break from doing everything else with your horse for one week. Your horse is on vacation - no lessons for one full week, no tacking up, no riding, no doing any major stuff. I want you to be with your horse and be just like another horse in the herd.

If you can do this for two weeks the rest of this process will go even smoother. So do what you can.

I want you to go out to the pasture and spend quality time together with both horses. That means you can do one of these two things:

1. Hang out and walk around the pasture with your horses. Stop and start when they do. Watch what they are watching. And observe all the wonderful things in nature that they see, smell, and hear every day. Be, not do.

   Don't hang all over your horse, don't be needy with

your horse's attention, and don't talk to or touch your horse too much. Give yourself and your horse space to just be in the same pasture enjoying the day together. Simply relax and enjoy each other's company.

Do what horses normally do when they are in the field together, and don't do much of anything. You can be close to your horse, far away, or in between, and this will still work. But remain in an area where you all can see each other and keep an eye on what's going on with the herd.

If you are close to your horse, remember to keep yourself safe and stay out of your horse's kick zone. As always, it is your responsibility to keep yourself safe, so please pay attention and stay alert to what's going on around you at all times.

2. If your horse can be groomed at liberty, without tack, you can do a little grooming while you're sharing the pasture with him. This gives you something small to do to pass the time without putting any pressure on your horse. If he decides to leave you, let him.

Something else could be sitting in a chair watching your horses and enjoying the sights, sounds, and smells of their world. But do not bring out your phone, computer, or any electrical devices. This will take your attention away from relaxing with your horses, and it will work against you.

You don't want to stare at your horses all the time either, as this will also serve to add pressure. I want you to relax, be calm, and be quiet. Be observant of what's around you and know where your horses are without staring at them all the time. They know where you are, and they don't need to pay attention to you all the time to know that.

Try to stay calm during this whole process. Being calm on the inside helps you remain calm on the outside... and it is the same with your horse. So before you go in to hang out with your horses, I want you to stop and double-check your feelings. Are you calm? Are you feeling relaxed? Are you walking slowly or quickly? Do you have one thing on your mind - your horse - or are you thinking of all the things going on in the rest of your life?

If you are not calm and relaxed, do not start this section or move on to the next section. Do something that brings you joy and relaxation. This may be meditation, breathing exercises, or something else. You must calm yourself before you can expect your horse to be calm. I've added a chapter, chapter 6, on breathing exercises to help you stay calm when needed.

<u>Note:</u> *For the rest of this lesson, I'm going to refer to the herd-bound horse as horse X and the second horse that is not herd-bound as horse Z. That way it will be easier to distinguish between the two horses in the lesson.*

Step II – Beginning the Separation –
1 week (4–6 times a week)

<u>Now for week 2</u>:

I want you to halter horse X (the one displaying the herd-bound behaviors) and take him out of the pasture. But just on the other side of the pasture gate. Then hang out there for only

10–15 minutes each time. You can do this a few times a day if you like. The more, the better.

I want you to use the same parameters as the first week for hanging out. But this time you and your horse only have two options:

1. You can stand or sit in a chair while your horse eats grass.
2. You can stand or sit in a chair while your horse eats hay or grain from a bucket.

Do not move on from this exercise until your horse is calm, quiet, and relaxed on the outside of the pasture gate.

<u>Note:</u> *If your horse, horse X, starts to act up, gets nervous, circles around you, or any of the other herd-bound behaviors, gently talk to him and try to calm him down. Once he is calm, even for a few seconds, put him back in the pasture with the other horse, horse Z. You can go to Chapter 7 to view techniques to help calm your horse down if you need ideas.*

By working with your horse, calming him down, and then putting him back in the pasture, he learns that you are listening to him. He also learns that when he does calm down, he is placed back in the pasture. By doing this, you are using Positive Encouragement to teach your horse that you hear him and want to work with him.

Let me describe in more detail what I mean when I talk about Positive Encouragement and how I use it.

I developed the term **Blended Encouragement** © to describe the use of both positive reinforcement and negative reinforcement in training horses, which I prefer to call Positive Encouragement and Negative Encouragement.

<u>Positive Reinforcement</u> - The addition of a pleasant stimulus to reward a desired response. For example, your horse comes to you when called and gets a treat.

<u>**Positive Encouragement** ©</u> - Takes positive reinforcement a step further by not only rewarding your horse for a desirable behavior but also encouraging further growth. For example, you give your horse a treat when he learns to push a ball on cue and then you add further love and scratches to encourage him to continue learning.

<u>Negative Reinforcement</u> - The removal of an unpleasant stimulus to reward a desired response. For example, rein tension is applied until the horse stops and the removal of the tension rewards the correct response.

<u>**Negative Encouragement** ©</u> - Goes beyond training using negative reinforcement by allowing your horse to feel safe and protected when it is appropriate. For example, if there are loud noises near the arena you're working in that are continually causing your horse to become alarmed, it's better for both of you to take him away from the noise rather than try to persist through it.

British researchers into horse behavior discovered that negative feedback helps shape learning best, while positive feedback best helps with retention.

In other words: use, application, and removal of pressure to teach your horse a lesson and treats or other rewards to help him remember the lesson.

But I'm not keen on the word reinforcement or the word feedback.

I find them too sterile, don't you?

Words have a huge impact on how we feel and our intentions are a very powerful force when working with our horses.

So I prefer to use the terms **Positive Encouragement** © and **Negative Encouragement** © in my training programs to help keep the whole experience positive, for both my horses and for me.

When I hear the word encouragement, my brain automatically thinks warm, happy thoughts, doesn't yours?

As we are using a mix of these 2 approaches, I have called this combination **Blended Encouragement** © as it helps the learning process by making the lessons both more enjoyable and easier to remember.

This also makes it a lot more enjoyable for me as a trainer to use as I can see how much happier it makes my horses. That is a top priority for me, to bring joy and happiness to my horses, which in turn improves my horse's health and well-being.

Right, back to solving the issue of herd-bound behavior…

Depending on their past experiences, most horses are used to being told what to do and that humans don't usually listen to what they are trying to say.

So by doing this Beginning the Separation exercise, you are telling your horse that you are different, that you can be trusted.

This one small action builds trust and confidence in your horse by showing him that you care about him and that you aren't a threat in any way. It's all positive. The threat he may currently be worrying about is that you are going to forcibly take him away from his buddy without his permission. His herd-bound behaviors are him telling you that he doesn't want this to happen.

This part should only take one week, but if your horse, horse X, is not calm and stands on the outside of the gate easily, continue this part for a second week. Remember, this chapter is the medium resolution. It gets a bit more complicated and longer with the higher severity of the problem. So take your time here, and the rest will come easier.

Note: _If you can't commit to these two weeks or you lose your motivation, keep asking yourself, "Do you really want to fix this problem?" If your answer is yes, then you can do this! If you need to wait to have a full two weeks available to do Steps I and II, then please wait. It makes a big difference._

Step III – Preferring to be with You – 1–2 weeks (4–6 times a week)

Now for week 3:

This week we are going to continue the routine you started in section I and II, hanging out with your horse inside the pasture for a short time while he remains calm and then hanging out outside the pasture for 10–15 minutes. But this week we are also going to add an exercise.

So once you hang out inside the pasture and outside by the gate for a bit and your horse, horse X is calm, we are going to take him for a short walk. At first this is just going to be a very short walk away from the gate. On days 1–3 of this section, I want you to focus on where your horse is comfortable and watch his reactions closely.

Once you are calm and your horse is calm, after hanging out for a bit on the outside of the pasture, ask him to pick up his head and walk just a bit further with you. We want him to remain comfortable, so only move a few feet away from the pasture. You can do either of the following:

1. You can choose to walk alongside the pasture fence line away from the gate.
2. You can choose to walk away from the gate but remain in view of the other horse, horse Z.

Do what is easiest at first. If walking the outside of the fence line is easy and the other horse walks with you, then do that. 'Push the Easy Button'. After moving a few feet away from the gate, let your horse stop and eat some grass. If you don't have grass, set up a few spots where you place grain, hay, or a few treats a few feet apart in advance.

You can even carry a bucket of treats or grain with you and put it down for your horse to eat from once you have moved. However, don't do this last part if you have a food-aggressive horse. Always keep yourself safe. You know your horse's reactions and what he will and won't do, so modify these steps if you need to. It's ok to do them in smaller, baby steps if you need to in order to keep yourself safe.

You want this experience to be fun for your horse. You want him to want to be with you instead of his buddy and enjoy the process. Your job is to stay calm and keep your horse calm during the walk. If he acts up, or even gets anxious or nervous, stop and turn around right away or back up a few steps until he is comfortable. Make sure to talk to your horse to reassure him that he is safe while going back to a spot where he is comfortable. Then relax there for a few minutes.

You want to change his focus away from leaving his buddy. So the focus is on you, what you're doing together, and the grass or the treats he is getting. Later, the focus will be on you and where you are going together.

His focus right now is on you and not walking too far away from the pasture and his buddy. So if horse X happens to start looking back at his buddy and whinnying, get his attention and refocus him on something else. The focus can be you talking to him, petting him, or giving him a treat.

However, if you can't get his attention and he starts to get more anxious, turn around or back up and get to a spot where he calms down and is happier. Try to go back to a spot where he is comfortable without going all the way back into the pasture. Even if you must go back to being outside of the pasture gate, that is okay for now.

For instance: Being outside the gate is spot A, three feet away is spot B, and then four feet away from that is spot C. If horse X can go to spot A and B without issue and then at spot C starts to get anxious and you can't calm him down, then go back to spot B until he's calm, and start from there. Don't go back to spot A unless he is also anxious and can't calm down at spot B.

You can even keep a few treats in your pocket, so when he gets back to a spot outside of the pasture where he is calm and settled, then give him a treat as positive encouragement. He did good because he didn't freak out and bolt, because he didn't get too upset and angry, and because he found a spot outside of the pasture where the two of you could be comfortable together.

Note: We don't want your horse to get treat dependent so only use them sparingly and only when it is a clear positive encouragement. Not just when they beg for it or expect it.

Every time you do this exercise, look at the positives and what you've accomplished, even if it is baby steps. Don't get frustrated if you can't go all the way around the farm on day 1. It will take some time for horse X to trust you, be reassured that you are working with him and listening to him, and that he chooses to be with you rather than horse Z.

His focus will shift to wanting to be with you over the other horse. Allow it to take the time it takes, and it will come naturally and organically. This way the results will last a lifetime, as long as nothing else changes, as you will see in the severe case.

After your horse has settled down and has eaten for a while (5–10 minutes) in his new spot, then try again, going a few more feet away together. Let him eat there for about 5–10 minutes, and again try moving a bit further out. Then again and again until you get to that spot where you know you're at that line in the sand and you don't want to push through it - which is a good thing! When your instincts say, *"This is good enough for today,"* then stop right there. We always want to end on a good note.

Don't Push!

The first day or so, you may only get to move away once or twice. That's fine. This is when you are learning to listen to where your horse is comfortable. And he is learning that you are paying attention to what he is telling you. It is a give-and-take right now, and you are learning to work together in a new situation.

Once you get to this last spot where he feels comfortable, hang out there together enjoying it for about 5–10 minutes. While your horse eats, you can pet him, reassure him with your words, and give him scratches. Watch your horse's ears and body language though. If talking to him or touching him makes his ears go back or he flinches and moves away from your touch, that means he doesn't want to be touched right now. Listen to his requests and don't touch him. This is when you want to reassure him, not annoy him.

Once you're done with this spot or he starts to get a bit anxious, start going back to the pasture. At first you will go back to each of your spots and then to the outside of the pasture gate (your first spot). Then stop there for a few minutes to get comfortable and eat a bit more. After all that, put him back in the pasture while he's calm and happy and before he gets anxious again.

Focus on being calm and relaxed (eating grass, scratches, giving treats, etc.). When you get back to the gate, you can also give horse X a treat and tell him thank you for being such a good boy. Then let him back into the pasture with his buddy.

While you are outside of the pasture, all your attention should be on horse X. You want him to feel extra special that he's with you and that you are all about him. It's the two-of-you-against-the-world kind of feeling. He's the special one that gets to come out and be with you for as long as the two of you are together, calmly doing this exercise.

Do this over and over, mixing it up with what you do at the stops to stay calm (add a massage or brushing). Really pay attention to your horse's body language, as this will tell you everything you need to know. The second he starts to get anxious, stop, calm him down, move a few steps back toward the gate, and start from there. Know the areas where your horse is comfortable and calm.

Another way to keep your horse X calm or focused when you leave the pasture is to start with small wins. Every time you take your horse X out of the pasture, place a bucket of grain, hay, or treats along the path beforehand that he can eat. Maybe just start with one or two and then add more in time so you can move further and further away.

Pretty soon your horse will look forward to leaving to get a treat and have his special time with you. And later the treats will become grooming time or scratches from you. *"Mom time"*, as I like to call it with my horses.

Do this every day for a week, or two weeks if you need. Do this exercise over and over and get further and further away each time if you can. Make sure your horse stays calm and is focused on something other than horse Z in the pasture.

As you get further and further away (always staying within eyesight of the pasture and the other horse), get more creative. Give the walks a purpose. Walk to something (a water trough, an arena, the barn, another horse, etc.) As you do this it will help make the walks longer and longer. However, now your horse X is focused on where the two of you are going and what the two of you are doing together instead of treats or the other horse.

Have an intentional endpoint in mind every time. If you get there, great! If not, that's okay, too, because eventually you will get there. Look at that spot and tell your horse that you are going over to it. As always, your intentions and what you focus on are super important. But if you need to stop part way there for grass or scratches, that's fine too.

I want you to *'Push the Easy Button'* here as well and keep both horses in sight of each other. This will set you up for success, not failure. And if you ever want to just hang out with your horse for an hour or so and do nothing else... that's more than acceptable. You can't hang out too much with your horse as every time you do this, you and your horse will naturally get closer and closer.

Once the above fix becomes easy and simple to do, you can start taking horse X farther away so the two horses cannot see each other. Follow the same instructions as above if your horse starts to get nervous once the other horse is out of sight. And little by little, your horse will no longer be herd-bound.

This concludes my medium herd-bound case and what worked for D'Artagnan.

<u>Note:</u> *Your horse will have good days and bad days just like you do. So if one day he decides he doesn't want to go as far as he did the day before, for whatever reason, respect his request, allow him his voice and don't push it. Let him decide where he is comfortable and not comfortable, and work with not against him. This is a two-way conversation, a give-and-take, so be flexible.*

Never forget to watch your horse's body language. If at any time he gets nervous or anxious, stop, calm him down, move back a few steps until he is calm, and then start from there. That means that it's your horse's choice where to start from and where to go. Your horse will let you know how far he can move away from the pasture or when he wants to move towards the pasture.

After he trusts you more, you can start making requests along the way and decide where the two of you are going. You can also switch it up some days. Just have fun with it and go slow. Trust doesn't happen overnight.

However, it is your choice when to stop the session. Once you feel that what you've both achieved in the session is enough, turn around and go back to the pasture. If your horse decides he wants to stop a few times to eat grass as you're going back, let that be his choice.

Just be flexible, calm, and patient. It will all work out.

CHAPTER
FOUR

How to Resolve a Severe Case of Herd-Bound Behavior

"It's never crowded along the extra mile."
WAYNE DYER

———————

My process for horses where only one is severely herd-bound – (Timeframe: 10 weeks)

Here is my severe case story:

In the first chapter, I discussed my worst-case scenario with Apollo. I won't go into that story again, as you've already read it, but this is the step-by-step process of what I did. It worked really well for us, and I hope that if you are in the same situation with your horse, it works just as well for you.

To begin with, you will start out the same as you would with a medium-severity case so please make sure you have read through that entire process before reading further here.

Because this case will take you longer to resolve, you really need to stay positive. Celebrate the wins, no matter how small, and just keep going. It may feel a bit slow at first, but it will quickly speed up, and the issues will be resolved in no time.

If you always keep the end result in mind, it will help you get through the tough days. You will have them and so will your horse. But at the end of this, you will both be more connected, have a deeper understanding of each other, and be much more comfortable and confident.

The first three steps are the same as in the Medium case in Chapter 3. The only difference is how long I want you to stay in each step. So I'm going to ask you to read the first three steps in the Medium case but adhere to the times I give you below.

Step I - Hit the Reset Button – 2 weeks (4–6 times a week)

For the first two weeks:

Follow Step I, **Hit The Reset Button,** instructions as outlined in Chapter 3, but instead of doing them for one week, do them for at least two weeks.

I want to make sure you have a definite connection started. When Apollo got so bad, our connection went out the window and all he could think about was not being with his buddy Harry.

If you can't feel a connection after two weeks, it's ok to continue this another week if you need to. Just as kids grow up and do things at different ages, horses learn at different speeds too so there is no pass or fail on how long these exercises take to do. They take as long as they take so you may as well just enjoy the journey.

And as I said earlier, if you ever want to just hang out with your horse for an hour or so and do nothing else... go right ahead!

Note: *If you and your horse are not calm and relaxed, do not move on to the next section. Go back and redo this section if needed.*

Step II – Beginning the Separation – 1 week (4–6 times a week)

This is where it starts to get a bit more complicated. Apollo was severely herd-bound to Harry, but he only pitched a fit when Harry left and Apollo had to remain in the pasture alone. Apollo was kind of okay with me taking him out of the pasture for a walk and leaving Harry in the pasture alone.

I say kind of okay because once he couldn't see Harry anymore, he'd start to act up and we would have to turn around. But when Harry left the pasture and was out of sight, Apollo's behavior got extremely out of hand and he became dangerous.

If you find that you need to modify a step here and there, please do so to keep yourself safe. You know your horse and your abilities, and not everything is going to be identical to how it was in Apollo's case. So please adjust if and when you need. Baby steps are fine in this process as long as you are moving forward and following the process properly.

However, don't move on to the next step until your horse is calm and confident with you and the situation. Be patient with both yourself and your horse. It may take two weeks or it may take four weeks, depending on how severe your case is.

Note: If you lose your motivation, keep asking yourself, "Do you really want to resolve this problem?" If your answer is yes, then you can do this! Be patient. It does work.

Now for week 3:

Follow Step II, **Beginning the Separation,** instructions as outlined in chapter 3. Then come back here and continue reading.

This part should only take one week, even in a severe case, but if your horse, horse X, is still not calm and doesn't stand on the outside of the gate easily, continue this section for another week.

It's worth taking your time here and getting it done properly so when you move on to the next step the results will last. When you complete this entire process you want the results to last a lifetime. Right? So don't rush through it.

Step III – Preferring to be with You – 1-2 weeks (4–6 times a week)

Now for week 4:

Follow Step III, **Preferring to be with You,** instructions as outlined in Chapter 3. Then come back here and continue reading.

This may only take one week if this is easy for you and your horse as it was with Apollo. Because, as I mentioned above, he didn't mind leaving Harry to go for walks with me. But your horse may be different.

If you feel the need to do this step one more week, go ahead. The more quality time the two of you spend together, the more your horse will trust you.

For example, we both were happy to go visit Apollo's other friend Ray as Apollo loved it and the activity changed his focus and at the same time rewarded him for his calmer behavior.

Go back to Step II or I when you feel the need, do what makes you and your horse comfortable. It's a give and take. Sometimes you may find you moved on too quickly to the next step and you need to give the prior step more time. This is completely normal and will actually help your progress faster than steaming ahead and forcing the issue.

I want you to *"Push the Easy Button"* here as well and keep both horses in sight of each other. This will set you up for success. Then once this becomes easy and simple to do, you can start taking your horse further away so the two horses cannot see each other. But that is the last step, so don't try that yet. Wait until we get to that section.

Step IV – Continuing the Separation – 2 weeks (4–6 times a week)

Now it's time to move past the Medium case and into the Severe case and to work with your horse and the other horse at the same time. You will need the help of someone else to work with the other horse, horse Z, at the same time you are working with your herd-bound horse, horse X.

Once you can take your horse X out and he is much calmer with being taken out of the pasture and walking away (still within sight of the other horse), then you can start to teach your horse that it's okay for him to do things on his own. When both of them are busy doing things on their own, with their focus on something else and still within sight of each other, they also learn that it's ok because they are safe.

Sometimes the herd-bound behavior is a lack of trust in their owner to protect them, and they feel the need for the protection of the herd (the other horse). Sometimes the herd-bound behavior is because they feel they are the one that needs to protect the herd because they don't feel there is strong leadership. Or vice versa, they feel they need the protection of the other horse because the environment is new and scary, as in Apollo's case.

Plus, in Apollo's case, his father Jazz and his buddy D'Artagnan had recently disappeared from his life and so he was probably feeling a profound sense of loss and loneliness. As a result, I think he was also afraid that when Harry left, he might not come back either and he would be all alone again.

So it's very important you seek to instill confidence, trust, companionship, leadership, protection, and friendship in your horse.

Do not move on from this exercise until your horse is calm, quiet, and relaxed while away from the other horse. But still in sight of each other.

Now for weeks 5-6:

Before you do this step, I still want you to hang out with your horse, just as in Step I, for about 5–10 minutes. I want you to connect and feel comfortable together before you actually do something. Do this at the beginning of every session. This will help your progress considerably.

You want to have both horses coming out of the pasture at about the same time, so they see each other doing things outside the pasture. However, every time you do this, your herd-bound horse, horse X, should come out first. Since he is already used to coming out and leaving the other horse, he will feel comfortable still coming out of the pasture first. This little detail means a lot and could be the difference between him acting out or not. **Do not skip this!**

Once you've spent 5–10 minutes just hanging out with both horses in the pasture, until your herd-bound horse is calm, put a halter on him. Then have someone else come in and put a halter on the other horse, horse Z. Do this every day you go out.

Take horse X out of the pasture and head off in one direction as if you were still in Step III. Then have someone else take the other horse out, horse Z, and go off in the opposite direction. You don't have to go far. At first you want to stay fairly close to each other. Take this part slowly.

At first let them both graze close by each other, and then move them a bit more apart and let them graze again. Keep doing this and get further and further apart, always still in view of each other. Give them at least 5-10 minutes at each grazing spot before adding more distance between them. You could even have little stops along the way with treats as you did in Step II as they graze further and further away from each other.

When your horse gets to a spot where he is now uncomfortable with the distance, stop both horses from going any further. Bring both horses closer to each other where your horse becomes calmer and comfortable again. Let them both graze for another 5 minutes or so, and then take them both back to the pasture and let them go. That is a good ending to the first few sessions. Keep doing this exercise until your horse is comfortable going further away and is no longer really concerned with the other horse, horse Z.

Your horse will learn that you are listening to him when he gets nervous or anxious and you are responding to and respecting his requests. This will instill in him a good deal of trust in you and it will also teach him that you will always take him back to his buddy, no matter what. There is no forced separation, there is no punishment when he shows you that he's worried, and you're not taking them away from each other forever. This will go a long way to reassure your horse and make him feel comfortable.

Once you can have them both further apart, you can do something fun with your horse and give him something to look forward to as you did on your earlier walks. Incorporate some of the same things to change his focus. Add a massage, go to the arena and play with a ball, go visit another horse, or do some grooming. The other person with horse Z can do the same thing wherever they are.

Once your horse is comfortable being far away but still in view of the other horse, then it's time to work on taking them out of each other's line of sight. Take this very slowly. If your horse starts to act up again, stop and take him back to a place where he is comfortable and relax for a few minutes. Again, change the focus. You may need to take him back to a spot where he can see the other horse, that's fine for now.

If you can get them out of sight of each other, even for a few minutes, that's great. If not, that's okay too for now. Don't push it. We are going to work more on that later. Try it here for a very short time.

Remember to start out with shorter distances with the two horses and then make the distance longer and longer. Also, don't wait until your horse acts up to turn around. One day go only six feet away, and if they are both okay, stop the session and go back to the pasture.

Note: _You don't want to wait until your horse acts up before you take him back to the pasture. It's actually better to_ _never_ _have him act up because if you wait until he does, then you're actually reinforcing a bad habit. You are teaching your horse that if he acts up, he gets to go back to the pasture to be with his buddy. You don't want that._

Some days when there is no reaction and you've stayed out grazing for 20–30 minutes with no incidents, just say "thank you," pet your horse, and take them both back to the pasture. You always want the whole process to be pleasant. If he starts to think that every time you take him out, you're taking him away from his buddy, he will learn not to want to go out with you. So always keep these excursions positive.

Even if your horse becomes just a little edgy, immediately react and listen to calm him down. You don't have to take him back to the pasture immediately, because then you're teaching him a bad habit again, not a good habit. Just go back a few steps until he is calm and continue grazing or grooming. That leaves you in control of when to end the session (on a good note) and go back to the pasture. That is your positive encouragement.

Step V – Continuing to be with You – 2 weeks (4–6 times a week)

Now it's time to work with your horse in the pasture while the other horse leaves the pasture.

<u>Weeks 7-8</u>:

Before you do this step, I still want you to hang out with your horse, just as in Step I, for about 5–10 minutes. I want you to connect and feel comfortable together before you actually do something. Do this at the beginning of every session. It's still very important.

In this step, you will need someone else to help you again, as they should take the horse without the herd-bound issue, horse

Z, out of the pasture, and you should stay in the pasture with your horse, horse X. But don't take the other horse out of the pasture until you are ready and have spent the time hanging out with both of them.

After you have been in the pasture with both horses and everyone is calm and happy, put a halter on your horse, but this time stay in the pasture. At first you may need to just keep him from running around too much when the other horse leaves. However, if your horse becomes too upset and starts kicking up or running circles around you and you can't calm him down, you need to think about your own safety.

That is the priority in this section - keep yourself safe and at a safe distance if your horse gets too unruly. Also, don't let the other person take horse Z too far away once they leave the pasture. Remember to *'Push the Easy Button'*.

Before your horse gets unruly, I want you to try these suggestions to help calm your horse down while the other horse leaves the pasture:

- Have some treats or grain for him to eat while the other horse leaves the pasture.
- Make being without the other horse more enjoyable by doing something your horse enjoys, like playing with a ball or walking up and down the pasture with you.
- Walk around the pasture together looking for the best patches of grass and stay near him when he eats.
- Have one or two other places in the pasture that have treats or hay lying around to walk to.
- Give him a massage or do some grooming.
- Do something your horse really enjoys and change his focus back to you.

Note: Make sure this process isn't the only thing you do with your horse, otherwise you will again be teaching him that every time you come to see him, the other horse will leave him, which will make him more anxious, not less. So in between these sessions, come into the pasture where they both are and do things there, either something he finds fun or just hanging out together.

Do this in segments so your horse can get used to the other horse leaving and coming back without issue. You will still have the two horses in sight of each other for now. Horse Z shouldn't go too far away at first.

Remember, you want this to be as pleasant as possible with positive encouragement. That means without the pain or anxiety of separation and all the herd-bound behaviors that go with it. You will probably still see these behaviors reappear here and there. But we are teaching your horse that it really is okay to be without the other horse for a little while because you are there to protect him. The herd-bound behaviors will get less and less and will eventually disappear.

I want to clarify what I mean when I talk about treats.

The majority of people think of treats as food, but they can be much more than that. I use various 'treats' in my programs in a variety of different ways but all of them are a form of positive encouragement.

For me, treats are anything that your horse enjoys. Food treats can be grain, hay, carrots, apples, mints, homemade cookies, etc. Non-food treats can be scratches, words of encouragement, hugs, love, grooming, etc.

Other treats can be just hanging out together, walking somewhere together, grazing together, riding on trails, playing with a ball, playing with another horse, or whatever your horse enjoys doing.

Use a mix of treats and a variety of types of treats so your horse doesn't become food aggressive, or treat dependent, or look at you as a 'Pez dispenser'. Your aim should always be to become the best partner and friend to your horse and vice versa. It's a two-way conversation.

Work it out together as a team and use treats when, where and how you need them. This is where trial and error come in and what you feel is the right balance between treats and results, trust and dependence.

When following the guidelines in each of these herd-bound cases and working on resolving your issues, use treats intermittently and only when you feel it is truly a **Positive Encouragement ©**.

You want to encourage and help your horse enjoy learning and being with you. You want to help your horse trust you and feel safe. And you want him to be focused on you and prefer being with you over other horses so he is no longer herd-bound.

Right, back to the process...

Part A. Repeat Step II with the opposite horse: (week 7)

Have the other person halter the other horse, horse Z (the one not displaying the herd-bound behaviors) and take him out of the pasture - just on the other side of the pasture gate. Have them hang out there for only 10–15 minutes each time. They can do this a few times a day if you like. The more, the better. You then stay in the pasture with your horse, horse X.

I want your friend with the other horse, horse Z, to use the same parameters as you did the first two weeks hanging out, but this time they have three options:

1. They can stand or sit in a chair while their horse eats grass.
2. They can stand or sit in a chair while their horse eats hay or grain from a bucket.
3. They can groom their horse on the other side of the gate or fence line.

Do not move on from this exercise until your horse, horse X, is calm, quiet, and relaxed while still in the pasture with you.

Note: If your horse starts to act up, gets nervous, circles around you, or any of the other herd-bound behaviors, gently talk to him and try to calm him down. You can also occupy his time and change his focus by giving him some hay or grain to eat. Once he is calm, after about 5 minutes or so, put the other horse back in the pasture with your horse. You should then spend some more time with both horses, so they both begin to look at you as part of the herd.

By working with your horse, calming him down, and then putting the other horse back in the pasture, you teach your horse that you are listening to him and that when he does calm down, he is placed back with his buddy. By doing this, you are using positive encouragement to teach your horse that you are listening and that you want to work with him and help him.

Plus, you are doing so much with the herd that you are beginning to become an integral member of the herd. You are also teaching your horse that having the other horse leave while you are around isn't such a bad thing. You are there and the focus is on you, so he doesn't need the other horse.

This part should only take one week, but if your horse needs another week, then please allow him the time he needs to understand you're only trying to help. Most of the time it will go quicker; however, don't move on any faster than one week.

Part B. Repeat Step III with the opposite horse: (week 8)

We are still hanging out first with both horses inside the pasture for a short time and then hanging out with the other horse just outside of the pasture for 10–15 minutes. However, this week we are going to add a little walk for the other horse, horse Z.

Once your horse, horse X, is calm inside the pasture, have the other person take the other horse, horse Z, for a short walk outside of the pasture while you and your horse remain inside the pasture. At first this is just going to be a very short walk away from the gate just as we did before with your horse.

On days 1-3 of this section, I want you to focus on where your horse is comfortable inside the pasture and watch his reactions closely. The other horse outside the pasture shouldn't have any issues, so you are watching your horse, which is inside the pasture with you.

Once your horse is calm, after hanging out for a bit, ask the other person to walk horse Z just a bit further away. We want your horse to remain comfortable, so just have the other horse move a few feet away from the pasture. Here are the two things they can do:

1. They can choose to walk alongside the pasture fence line away from the gate.
2. They can choose to walk away from the gate but remain in view of the horse in the pasture.

Do what is easiest at first. If walking the outside of the fence line is easy for your horse to handle, then do that. *'Push the Easy Button'*. After the other horse moves just a few feet away from the gate, let him stop and eat while your horse stays calm. Remember, you can keep treats, hay, or grain inside the pasture on the ground, so your horse has something better to do than be focused on where the other horse is going.

You want this experience to be fun for your horse without too much stress. You want him to want to be with you instead of his buddy and enjoy the process. Your job is to stay calm yourself and to keep your horse calm while in the pasture. If he acts up, or even gets anxious or nervous, ask the other person with the other horse to stop and turn around or back up a few steps until your horse is more comfortable.

Make sure to talk to your horse to reassure him that his buddy is still around and that they are both safe. You want to instill confidence and trust in your horse.

You want to try and change the focus again, so the focus is on you and what you're doing together in the pasture, like the grass or the treats he is getting. You can also change the focus by walking in the pasture together. You should keep the halter on in this step.

The focus right now is on you and him. So don't walk too far away from his buddy but try to change the focus to what you are doing, not what his buddy is doing. If your horse happens to start looking around for his buddy and whinnying, just get his attention and refocus him on something else. He can look at his buddy, just not 100% of the time.

The focus can be on you talking to him, petting him, or giving him a treat. You could even start by walking both horses together but on the opposite sides of the fence line.

Note: It is really important to have a halter on your horse, horse X, while the two of you are in the pasture together and his buddy is leaving to go on short walks. This is because most horses, when they have a halter on, know that they are supposed to "do" something with you. This one simple act helps increase their focus on what you are doing and decreases their focus on what their buddy is doing.

If you allow him to stay in the pasture without a halter, he will focus only on his buddy leaving, and you are at higher risk of getting hurt because he won't care that you're in there with him. However, if he is too dangerous, you can tie him safely to a fence pole, barn pole, or something else where he can safely move around but not run you over or kick you. But you don't want him wrapping himself around a pole either. Keep it safe for both of you.

Note: When he becomes calmer, you could also put a halter on your horse without the lead rope if you feel he will stay with you. This is usually better to do in your second or third week working on this step. You can use other things to keep his attention on you instead of the other horse. However, if he acts up, put the lead rope back on.

If you can't get his attention and he starts to get more anxious, ask your friend to bring the other horse back to a spot where your horse begins to calm down and is happier. However, try to get the other horse back to a spot where your horse is comfortable without coming all the way back into the pasture. Even if the other horse has to go back to just outside of the pasture gate, that is okay for now.

Every time you do this exercise, look at the positives and what you've accomplished, even if it is baby steps. Don't get frustrated if your friend can't take the other horse very far on day 1.

It will take some time for your horse to trust you, be reassured that you are working with him and listening to him, and he chooses to be with you rather than the other horse. Allow it to take the time it takes, and it will come naturally and organically. And some days you may go a little backwards, but then after another day it will go better than you expect. Be patient.

This was the hardest part for Apollo. But once he realized Harry wasn't going to go far away or out of sight, he calmed down quickly. This worked out within two weeks.

If it gets to the point where your horse is too upset when his buddy leaves and gets too far away, then leave the other horse at a closer spot, let them both eat and relax, and then ask your horse, inside the pasture, to walk farther away. So instead of moving the other horse away, move your horse inside the pasture farther away while the other horse remains in the same spot.

Be creative, thoughtful, and observant, and adjust where and when your horse needs it.

After your horse has settled down and has eaten for a while (5–10 minutes) in a new spot, then try again, going a few more feet away. Let him eat there for about 5–10 minutes, and again try moving a bit further away from his buddy who is outside the fence. Then again and again until you get to that spot where you know you're at that line in the sand and you don't want to push through it. This is a good thing! When your instincts say, "This is good enough for today," then stop right there. We always want to end on a good note.

Again, Don't Push!

You can also do other things like:

- Walking over to a ball that he likes to play with.
- Walking around the pasture looking for good grassy areas.
- Standing still and grooming him.
- Having your horse eat grain from a bucket while you clean the area close to him.
- Walking over to get some water.

After you're done with the session, put the other horse back into the pasture while your horse is calm and happy. When you are doing this, all your attention should be on your horse. You want him to feel extra special that he's with you and that you are all about him.

Another way to keep your horse calm or focused when the other horse leaves the pasture is to start with small wins. Every time the other person takes the other horse, horse Z, out of the pasture, have a bucket of grain, hay, or treats that your horse can eat. Pretty soon he will look forward to the other horse leaving just to get a treat and have his special time with you. When the other horse is back in the pasture, remove the treats just as I did in the Mild case scenario.

Do this step every day for a week, or two weeks if you need. Do this exercise over and over and get further and further away. Make it fun for both of you. Make sure your horse stays calm and is focused on something else other than the other horse outside of the pasture.

As you get further and further away (always staying within eyesight of the other horse), get more creative. Give the walks a purpose and walk to something (a water trough, the barn, another horse on the fence line, etc.) As you do this, it will help make the walks get longer and longer for both horses.

I want you to *'Push the Easy Button'* here as well and keep both horses in sight of each other. This will set you up for success. Then once this becomes easy and simple to do, you can start taking the other horse farther away so the two horses cannot see each other. But that is the last step. Don't try that until you read the next section.

Once you feel that what's been done is good enough for this session, you can call the other person back with the other horse and have them both in the pasture together again. After the session is over, remain in the pasture with both horses for at least 5–10 minutes just to hang out and be a part of the herd again.

Step VI - Out of Sight, Out of Mind - 2 weeks (4–6 times a week)

It's time to finish the process with your horses to get them completely un-herd-bound.

The finishing touches...

Now for weeks 9–10:

Before you do this step, I still want you to hang out with your horse, just as in Step I, for about 5–10 minutes. I want you to connect and feel comfortable together before you actually do something. Do this at the beginning of every session. It's still very important.

You've already gone for walks with your horse, horse X, outside of the pasture while horse Z stayed inside the pasture, and you've done the opposite. However, during each of those sessions, the two horses were always in sight of each other.

Now we are going to do those two exercises again but this time out of sight of each other.

Part A. The progression of Step III: (week 9)

Take the first week and start going for walks together again where your horse, horse X, is on the outside of the fence. This should be much easier now, as he will remember he is safe and will be focused on you. You didn't make him leave his buddy last time, so he won't be thinking about it too much.

However, you are now going to start taking your horse places where he can't see his buddy. Ease into this by going for short walks on day 1 and 2 and then making them longer. Even though the herd-bound behaviors have resolved when you go on short walks, from the first part of this lesson, once you start going places where your horse can't see the other horse, you will see the herd-bound behaviors start to reappear, at least to some degree. Don't worry. This is normal and will dissipate quickly.

Once your horse is comfortable and happy to go out with you for your special time together, still in view of the other horse, but further away now, I want you to start thinking about where you can go where the two horses are out of sight of each other.

It may be a building or a barn that separates them from sight or just around a corner. As a treat, right around that new corner, you can leave a bucket of food that is a pleasant surprise for your horse. Go someplace just a bit further than the last place your horse was comfortable going.

Do the same procedure you did in Step III, but this time you're going to progress out of sight of the other horse, and then just hang out there for a bit. Make it a very short period of time at first and then make it longer and longer each session. Make sure you separate sessions by doing them on different days.

Pick someplace that if your horse gets anxious, he can just poke his head around the corner of that building, or tree line, to see his buddy. That way he knows that he can easily see his buddy when he wants to. Stay here for a bit and then go right back to a comfortable location where he can see his buddy. This should be a simple transition.

Do this exercise a few times until it is no big deal to be out of sight. Then move further away in the same fashion as you did in Step III. Continue doing this for a few days or weeks, until your horse is no longer concerned about being out of sight of the other horse.

When your horse starts to get anxious or nervous, instantly calm him down and start to take him back to a place where he is comfortable and hang out there for a bit. You may lose some ground here and there on the first few tries and you may need to take him back to the outside of the gate to reassure him. That is fine. You will gain the lost ground back quickly.

Your horse just needs to trust that you are listening and that when he gets nervous, you will notice and do something about it without pushing him to do something that makes him feel pressured or punished. By this time you will be much better at knowing when he's uncomfortable and even be able to feel it coming on before he acts up.

Once you can do this with ease, go for walks that take your horse to a place that is out of sight of the other horse. Take him to a special place with hay or to another horse that he likes to talk to. If your horse trusts you and you take him places he enjoys going, he will stop the herd-bound behaviors because he will be focused on you.

I still don't want you riding your horse out of sight yet for safety reasons. Keep this to just walking together with a halter and lead rope. Once the herd-bound behaviors are resolved completely, then you can do this while riding.

Even when you start riding, always remember to keep watching your horse's body language. If at any time he gets nervous or anxious, or you feel it coming on, stop and calm him down. Do the same thing riding as you did on the ground.

When you're doing this section and working on getting your horse used to being out of sight of the other horse, start with being out of sight for a short time at first. Then as he gets used to it, trusts you more and is calmer longer, the walks out of sight can get longer and longer. Remember scratches, verbal "good boys," and grooming or petting are also treats and positive encouragement. It doesn't always have to be food. It shouldn't always be food. Mix it up.

Part B. The progression of Step III with the opposite horse: (week 10)

Now that your horse is happy to leave the pasture and go for long walks with you and doesn't care that he can't see the other horse anymore, it is time to stay in the pasture with your horse and let the other horse leave the pasture and get out of sight.

This was tougher for Apollo. Because this is where your horse could get more aggressive and dangerous as Apollo did in this section, I want you to have your phone on you and have the person taking the other horse out to also have a phone. This way if the other horse gets too far away and your horse starts to get too anxious, you can call the other person and ask them to start coming back.

Note: *This does work, and even though Apollo seemed worse the first few times I did this, he got better very quickly. Stay positive and keep going. You will get through this and so will your horse. If you stop here, it won't get better, and you'll still have a herd-bound horse. Don't stop!*

If your horse acts up at this point just like Apollo did, then go slowly and do things in baby steps. Keep yourself and your horse safe. If the other horse can only go out of sight for a short time, that's fine. You can work on this over and over and increase the distance and the amount of time the other horse is away.

This time you and your horse will stay in the pasture and the other horse, horse Z, will leave the pasture and move out of sight. However, keep the communication open between you and the other person just in case you need to ask them to come back in sight to help your horse ease into this section.

If your horse starts to get too anxious or nervous, just have the other horse come back towards the pasture until your horse has calmed down. Then allow the other horse to walk further away and go back and forth as needed.

Make sure you halter your horse before the other horse leaves the pasture and starts to walk off. You can do lots of things with your horse in the pasture to keep his focus on you instead of the other horse not being there.

- Put down a bucket of treats, hay, or grain for him to eat while you hold the lead.
- Walk around the pasture with him looking for a good patch of grass to eat.
- Groom him where he is comfortable, but only if he is calm enough to groom.
- Just hang out together enjoying nature and your surroundings.
- Clean the pasture or pull weeds together walking around on a lead or while your horse is tied.

It's funny, you can do the same thing in a different location, and even though your horse was fine with leaving his buddy, he may not be fine with his buddy leaving him. This is what happened with Apollo.

So look at each segment of this as something new that your horse may or may not be anxious about and be patient. His nervousness might not make sense to you, but it does to him. Let him have his voice and work with his insecurities to reassure him and develop more trust with him. This will go a long way, not only in resolving herd-bound issues, but it will also naturally and organically resolve some other issues at the same time.

Start this section off with both horses in sight and gradually go to being out of sight. Allow the progression to be natural and smooth for your horse.

Do these sections over and over, mixing it up with what you do at the stops to stay calm (add a massage or brushing), and give the walks a purpose. Walk to something (a water trough, an arena, the barn, another horse, etc.) Make it fun, and as you do, you can make the walks longer and longer. Before you know it, you'll be able to go on walks and rides with your horse without a problem.

All this is done with the halter on. Once he's much much better the final test is to take the halter off and make sure he doesn't start running around the pasture when his buddy leaves. But you can test here and there by taking only the lead off when the two of you are in the pasture without the other horse to see if he remains calm. If not, put the lead back on and continue working together.

Once you're comfortable with the two horses being out of sight while you're inside the pasture, the other person could even take their horse, horse Z, for a ride. Just remember to keep your phones with you just in case you need to call the other person and ask them to bring their horse back in sight.

This worked for me and Apollo and before long we were riding around the trails alone while Harry was off riding with his owner without any issues. It was beautiful to have our loving and trusting relationship back in place again.

We were able to have fun together, just the two of us again. Both of us were confident in the other again and we both felt safe. And I certainly didn't mind that he now enjoyed my company over that of other horses! That is how I came up with the idea of him being "herd-bound to me", and I was loving every second of it. All the love and attention with none of the bad behaviors and totally focused on our relationship together. Total bliss.

What to Do When You Have Two Horses That are Herd-Bound to Each Other?

"You'll see it when you believe it."
WAYNE DYER

My process for two mildly herd-bound horses. If both of your horses are herd-bound to each other and you are trying to fix this by yourself, here is a solution that has worked for me with Jazz and Apollo when I finally decided to take each horse on long trail rides alone.

Take the horse with the worst case of herd-bound behavior, horse X, out of the pasture and follow the steps in the chapter about mild herd-bound behavior. But when you take horse X out of the pasture, just stay at the gate at first and give horse Z food to keep him occupied and happy while you're on the other side of the fence.

Staying in the Pasture

You want horse Z to realize that when his buddy leaves the pasture, he gets goodies. But when you take horse X back into the pasture, remove the goodies that you gave horse Z. So not only does he get goodies when the other horse leaves the pasture, but he learns that when the other horse comes back into the pasture, he loses his goodies. That way he will start to prefer that the other horse leaves and stays out, so he has time to eat all the goodies himself.

As you've seen over and over in the instructions, hang out with both horses for a while first, and then start small, and naturally get further and further away from the pasture, being very alert of your horse's feelings and actions.

The other thing you need to watch when you are working with two herd-bound horses is that when the horse in the pasture starts to act up, give him a moment to run around safely, and then start to go back a few feet with the horse you took out until horse Z has calmed down a bit. You'll be working with and observing two horses at the same time and working with keeping them both calm. It's a bit tougher working alone with two horses, but it can be done.

It's a bit harder because one horse may get better faster than the other, and you'll have to adjust what you do, how far you go, and who gets what treats by listening to and observing their behavior and body language.

Your main focus here with two horses is to make sure that the horse in the pasture, horse Z, has less herd-bound behaviors and is comfortable first. That way, once he is comfortable with you leaving with horse X, you can then focus on horse X's herd-bound behaviors.

That means that the adjustments are all about horse Z in the pasture to start. When he stops eating or gets nervous, pause and let horse X eat grass (as long as he is comfortable there) and see if horse Z starts to calm down because you have stopped moving away. If not, move a few steps or a few feet closer and stop and pause again. Keep doing this until the horse in the pasture calms down a bit and starts eating again. Stay in this spot for a while and start from there.

<u>Note:</u> *Remember to 'Push the Easy Button', and if you need to, walk down the fence line on the outside of the fence so horse Z can follow along without issue.*

You can try to move a few more feet away from the pasture to see where and when horse Z gets anxious again, stop and pause, and then take a few steps closer until horse Z calms down again. Continue to do this until horse Z in the pasture can be without horse X for a bit and then focus on horse X. You may need to still watch horse Z to adjust where and when you need to stop, since you're working with two horses on your own.

Leaving the Pasture

Now that horse Z is calm and content to remain in the pasture with his goodies while you take horse X out for a walk, it's time to continue horse X on Step I of the Medium herd-bound instructions in Chapter 3. Start from the beginning. This will allow you to focus on only one horse at a time and get him comfortable being out with you while the other horse remains in the pasture. Do everything in Steps I, II, and III with horse X.

Switching Horses

Okay, you're almost done. That is, if you are trying to heal two horses with herd-bound behavior to each other and doing it by yourself. By this point you've completed the Mild case with horse Z and the Medium case with horse X. And horse X is good now going off with you and horse Z is good being in the pasture by himself.

All done, right? Nope!

It doesn't always translate the same when you switch horses. You've got horse X all done, so you can take him out to ride and go on walks, and the two of you are great on your own together. But now you want to take horse Z out for a ride without horse X.

If you're very lucky you have two extremely smart horses on your hands. So when you take horse Z out, he realizes that it's a similar situation, and he gets to now be out with you and go on special trails and walks. However, 9 out of 10 times this is not the case.

The nice thing is that once you start again from square one, Step I of the Medium case, your horse Z will catch on quickly and probably even quicker than your horse X did.

Just do the same thing with the second horse, horse Z, that you did with the first horse, horse X, and you will soon have two horses you can take out anytime you want. They will understand that it's a special time with you, they'll enjoy it, and you all will have fun.

Make sure you spend quality time with the horse that's left in the pasture when all three of you are back together. We don't want one getting jealous of the other. They both need their special time with you and to be able to play, whether that is in the pasture or outside the pasture.

Even though Jazz and Apollo and I were usually together on trails for years, after I did this fix, I could take either one out for a long ride alone without any issues. I never had to do it again. The results lasted the rest of their lifetimes.

Breathing Techniques to Calm Yourself Down

*"Happiness is something that you are, and
it comes from the way you think."*
WAYNE DYER

Here is a breathing technique that I use that helps me calm down. I hope it does the same for you.

- After a day of stress, I take a moment when I get to the barn to stop before I go to my horses.
- I find a spot that feels good to me and is private.
- I intentionally begin to think calming thoughts and get myself centered.
- I first close my eyes and let go of the day's stresses or problems.
- I take a deep breath in and count to 4 as I'm breathing in.
- Then I hold that breath for a count of 5.

- I let it out for a count of 6, and then I repeat that process.
- I breathe in through my nose, and out through my mouth.
- Breathe deeply from the diaphragm (lower abdomen) rather than shallow breathing from the chest.
- Listen to the sounds of nature.
- Do this 10 times or until you have calmed down.
- Think of nothing but letting go of all the stress and taking in all the nature around you.
- Feel the positive energy coming in and the stress leaving your body.
- Think and believe that everything else in your life can wait until you've spent quality time with your horse.
- During your time together, your focus should be only on you and your horse.

Here is a link to a video showing this technique:
https://teddiezieglerhorsemanship.com/breathing-technique/

Once you're calm and ready to be with your horse, here is a quick tip that will help you remain calm and also help you connect quickly to your horse.

Learning to relax, quieting your brain and allowing yourself to just be with your horses can be tricky. But this is what I teach and how I allow my horse to connect with me on his terms and start our session off on a good note.

People grow and change over the years, and so does your horse. Each session or new training can bring about a new phase in your relationship. I want you and your horse to get to know each other again. Learn to start each session on the right foot. I like to say it is like a second honeymoon or going on vacation without the kids.

The pasture is your horse's safe area because he is free to do what he wants and to be natural without any halter or tack. But you also want to let your horse know that even with you in his pasture, it is still a safe area for him to be his authentic self.

To your horse, it really doesn't become his shared safe area until he realizes that you are not going to ask him to do anything or force him to act in a certain way. Most horses think something along the lines of, *"Oh no, here she comes again. What is she going to ask me to do today?"*

But if you want your horse to view your arrival with a *"Yippee, here she comes! Let's have some fun"* kind of reaction and treat you as an integral member of the herd, then you need to act like you're a part of the herd. Which means not immediately forcing your horse to do anything or even forcing him to accept your touch.

So many people go out and automatically start to pet their horse and don't realize or notice when their horse shies away from their touch or pins their ears when they raise their hand to pet them. To a horse, you are forcing your touch on him. You may not think it's forcing, but he might not be ready for it. Give him the choice and watch his reactions. Some days he might not be in the mood to be touched and other days he may nuzzle into you to cuddle.

Don't you feel like that some days?

What we are seeking is a two-way conversation. You want your horse to come to you if he wants to. Let him check you out and not be forced to be with you. By allowing him to come check you out without any pressure, you are giving your horse the opportunity to get to know who you truly are inside. Let him sniff you and touch you without touching him. Watch how this changes his perspective and allows him the choice.

You might not feel that petting your horse is pressure, but if he doesn't want to be touched that day, then it is pressure to him. You'll be able to see this in his ears. If you reach out to pet him and his ears go back, stop. He doesn't want to be touched.

Just the opposite can happen too. You can go out with the intention of not petting your horse unless he asks for it, and he gives you his neck and looks at you asking for you to scratch him. That's great! That's him talking to you and telling you he wants your touch.

Let's just give him the benefit of the doubt and allow him to let you know when he is ready. Try it for one day. Go out to him but deliberately avoid touching him for the whole day and see what happens, see what he tells you. I promise you; you will see a difference.

You should wait for your horse to start the conversation with you. That may take a few hours, a few days, or maybe a few weeks. However, normally it only takes a few hours. Your horse must feel relaxed and safe in your presence and in his surroundings before he will start a conversation with you. Let him make the first move.

Watch his body language very closely and you'll be able to see the difference. When you start to walk up to your horse, if you see his ears go back for even a second, then stop. That shows you that he has reservations about your body language. When he does this, focus on just being together, doing nothing, and enjoying your surroundings, happy and peaceful together.

Even if your horse comes up to you because it is his habit to check in, allow him to touch you and sniff you without you touching him. As I suggested, try it for just one day. I know it's going to be hard, but it will be well worth it. It will also help you calm down by not having an agenda. Just be happy doing nothing together.

Even though it is important not to have any time demands, expectations, or agendas, I do want you to have the intention of wanting to be a part of your horse's herd, of relaxing and being happy.

However, being relaxed and happy does not mean being oblivious. I also want you to be aware of your surroundings and alert so you can keep yourself and your horse safe.

One of the basic protocols of a herd is to watch out for one another. You do this by being aware of your surroundings, noticing any possible threats, and being attentive to each other's needs.

When you do this right after you've done the breathing exercises to calm you down, and you start your session when your horse is ready, the rest of whatever you do together will go much smoother.

The little things make a big difference!

Techniques to Calm Your Horse

"Our intention creates our reality."
WAYNE DYER

How to help calm your horse down when he gets nervous or anxious:

<u>For your horse:</u>

1. Keeping yourself calm helps keep your horse calm. You can do this by using the breathing technique lesson in the chapter above or other calming techniques that you know yourself.
2. Groom your horse in a gentle, soothing way and find his favorite spots to make him feel comfortable. Move slowly, no quick actions or high hands.
3. Use your words in a soft and gentle manner to reassure your horse that he is safe with you to calm him down.

4. Stand in front of your horse's head so you are facing each other. Then put your hands on either side of his head on the lower part of the halter and slowly bend down at the waist and knees, pulling your horse's head down with you.

   a. Don't stand too close to his head. If he raises his head quickly, you should be far enough away that he won't hit your head.

   b. You want to have a steady, slow, and gentle pull for about five seconds, and then release the pull, but continue to hold onto the halter. Then do it again for another five seconds. If your horse moves his head down with you, only bring it down about 4–6 inches and then slowly release the halter. If he puts his head up again, repeat this procedure. This should relax your horse from an alert, highly-strung position, and over time he will see that he can safely let his guard down and relax around you.

5. Slowly stroke or scratch your horse with your hand and reassure him again with your voice, but don't hit or pat him. Patting is not something that horses do to each other naturally in the wild. However, stroking or scratching mimics the way a horse might rub against another horse in the wild, and it's the best way to soothe an anxious horse and get him used to your touch.

   a. Make sure to do this in a location where you know he is comfortable. For instance, my horse feels safe when I stand next to his front shoulder and look off in the same direction as he is while I scratch his shoulder. It's the two of us together against whatever spooked him. When I do this, he calms down immediately.

6. Use your index finger to gently stroke the groove that runs down the top of your horse's muzzle. Stroke gently and run your finger down the entire length of the muzzle. Rub from top to bottom. This can be incredibly relaxing for some horses. Only do this if your horse is already comfortable with you touching his face. Again, be careful not to have your face too close to your horse just in case he moves his head quickly.

7. If your horse is comfortable with you touching his face, you can try the following technique. Stand in front of your horse and gently rub the top of his nose. Once he brings his head down a bit, using both thumbs, gently rub the front of his forehead. Rub from inside to outside with your other fingers on the side of his head. Your palms should be above your horse's eyes, so you don't cover his eyes. Be very aware of where your head is compared to his head. We don't want any accidental head bumps here.

8. If your horse is not comfortable with you touching his face, you can do this technique. Stand to one side of your horse next to his mane. Put both hands gently on the top of his neck (wherever he will allow you to start) and gently rub back and forth with both hands going in the opposite direction. Intermittently add a gentle squeeze to the top as well. You are massaging your horse's neck at the top of his mane and going from the top (close to the ears) down toward the front shoulders. Do this in one sitting and in one session without taking your hands away. Think happy thoughts and calm yourself down

using your breathing techniques at the same time. This will help both of you stay relaxed and calm.

These techniques have all worked for me with all of my horses, so I hope you find one or two that also work for you and your horse. Being calm and happy together helps everything else you do together. It's a must for a good relationship and a good training session.

Here is a link to a video showing these techniques:
https://teddiezieglerhorsemanship.com/calming-techniques/

CHAPTER
EIGHT

What to Do if You're Not Sure the Problems are Related to Herd-Bound Behavior

"When you dance, your purpose is not to get to a certain place on the floor. It's to enjoy each step along the way."
WAYNE DYER

Sometimes herd-bound behavior doesn't look like herd-bound behavior.

Let me explain what I mean.

Whenever I am presented with a challenge with an unfamiliar horse, I always look to see if there is a core issue behind the behavior the horse is displaying. Sometimes the core issue has been there so long that it has been compounded and hidden so the problems presenting are not necessarily what the real core issue is.

Let me illustrate with a story about Dave and his horse Bob.

Bob had a happy home on a ranch with other horses... until his owner passed away. That one event changed his life and sent him down a pathway that turned him into a defensive, dangerous horse.

He was sent to a rescue facility with strange people and new horses and put in a small corral. His first reaction was to holler for his buddies and run around to try to get back to his owner and his buddies.

This then turned into sadness, confusion, and resentment for those he felt took him away from his happy home and his family. Bob's next reaction was biting, kicking, not listening to requests, and trying to ignore his captors.

Once Bob started down this path, he got yelled at, punished and beaten. This just made him both defensive and aggressive, and dangerous to be around. I'm sure you can understand how and why this happened. Bob no longer trusted humans and didn't want anything to do with them because in his eyes they were the cause of all his issues.

The rescue facility had too many horses in fact and so decided to sell the ones that were too difficult at the local horse auction. People went there to buy a cheap horse but the real cost was the emotional or physical issues these horses often had.

The horses that did not manage to find a new home were generally the ones considered dangerous and more often were the ones who would end up at the proverbial 'glue factory.' The man buying these horses also preferred them bigger and all of this described Bob perfectly.

Through no fault of his own, he had found himself at the auction with lots of people and loud noises so he was beside himself with fear and anger and was literally fighting for his life. He seemed like a perfect fit for the factory guy.

Luckily for Bob though, that day an old cowboy named Dave happened to drop by the auction. As soon as he saw the sadness and desperation in Bob's eyes, he connected with him right away.

Dave knew in his heart that this horse had a loving, kind self somewhere inside, and he wasn't going to let him go to the slaughterhouse. So when it came down to bidding against the 'glue factory' buyer, Dave wouldn't give in and eventually won.

Dave was delighted but at the same time thought, *"Great, but how am I going to train a big, dangerous horse like this?"*

He had been around horses for years and had owned lots of them before Bob but didn't currently have any so Bob found himself all alone on Dave's farm.

Dave tried his best and did everything he knew to help Bob. He had started learning natural horsemanship with a very well-known trainer but couldn't make it work with Bob. So he called in the trainer to see if he could help. No good. The trainer even called in his teacher to try and solve Bob's issues but to no avail.

Dave was persistent though and hired several other trainers, hoping that they could find the kind, loving horse in Bob that Dave knew lay hidden beneath all the anger and distrust.

The problem was that no one had addressed the <u>root cause</u> of all the issues. Instead, they tried to fix the problems that they saw, like the kicking and the striking out.

Besides not looking at the root cause of the problem, there was a large emotional issue that needed to be addressed: **fear.**

<u>Note:</u> *In 1994 Joseph E. LeDoux, professor of science at New York University, discovered that once established, a fearful reaction is relatively permanent. And this fear response can*

reappear spontaneously or can even be reinstated by an unre-lated stressful experience.

In other words, horses have a fear memory that can be turned on like a light switch, and this is what was happening to poor Bob. His past traumas had scarred him, and these fear emotions were being triggered when Dave and other trainers continued to treat him as a difficult and dangerous horse. Each action fed off of another and escalated Bob's emotions every time.

The results were predictable, some of the suggestions the trainers made worked in the short-term, only for Bob to revert later to his aggressive, defensive stance.

Everyone told Dave that Bob was a difficult or disobedient horse and a lost cause as none of them could fix him.

The truth was that Bob was alone and missing his family and friends - his original herd. His core issue was that he was still herd-bound to his original pasture mates after he had been ripped away from them.

Dave was so frustrated that he couldn't find an answer but he really wanted to help Bob. He decided that even if he couldn't ride him, he still wanted to make him happy.

He was stumped and was just about to give up when a friend suggested he call me. He told me I was his last chance with Bob. Every other trainer had told him to give Bob away or put him down because he was *"too difficult and was never going to change."*

We talked for a while over the phone and we scheduled a three-day private clinic together.

I drove six hours to meet Dave and as soon as I set eyes on Bob I could see what the issue was. Bob was a large, stocky thoroughbred, beautiful, strong and very proud. He was a fighter who wasn't going to take any crap from anyone. I knew why Dave had fallen for him.

I asked Dave about Bob's background and the sad story that followed just confirmed what I had already seen in Bob's eyes. I could see and sense the sadness and distrust Bob carried around. It was heartbreaking to witness this magnificent horse reduced to a shadow of his former self. Bob was not a happy horse.

Even though Dave and many others had been trying to do what they felt was best, another solution was called for.

I have a favorite saying to teach my students how to look at the problem differently in order to come up with a new solution. I call it, *"turning the world upside down."* Sometimes you need to turn the world upside down to figure out how to *'Push the Easy Button'*.

So, what did I suggest Dave do?

The first day we just hit the reset button, and the three of us did nothing but just hang out together. Our sole focus was on the connection between horse and human.

As you can perhaps imagine, Dave was a bit confused by this approach, especially as he was paying me and didn't expect us to be sitting around for the first third of our time together. He thought we ought to be doing something, that we should be training Bob.

However, that's exactly what we were doing. If done properly, you'd be surprised how much good doing nothing with your horse can do for the two of you!

The second day we worked on communication through herd dynamics and natural herd behaviors. This is the second of the three stages to gaining your horse's cooperation and a connection through familiarization in my RC3 approach.

Bob completely got it and understood what we were trying to do. By the end of that day he had totally changed, and his ferocious former self was replaced by this sweet, fun-loving fellow.

Dave got it too. When I saw him tear up at the end of our second day together, I knew he could feel a connection with Bob that he had never felt in all the three years that he had been trying to unearth the real Bob.

By the end of day three, Dave was able to put a halter on Bob, lead him around, ground tie him, and groom him without any issues. No more biting, kicking, striking, or bolting. The aggression and the resentment were gone. Bob was so happy that he had found a human that understood him and wanted to be a partner and a friend. More than that though, he had learned to trust again and understood that Dave only wanted the best for him.

I gave Dave a lot of tools to work with, my online program to follow, and more one-to-one help over the phone. Within a month, he was able to get a saddle and bitless bridle on Bob. Dave didn't even know if Bob had been ridden before, but the two of them were able to hit the trails the first time asking because of the respect and trust they had built between themselves.

Dave has never had another issue with Bob since. He can't believe what an amazing jewel Bob now is and how far he has come in such a short time. Dave says it's as if that period of Bob's life where he was aggressive and dangerous has now been left on the cutting room floor of his life. He is and always was this great, loving, kind, gentle horse.

I just love a happy ending, don't you?

This was an example of a horse that had been herd-bound either in a mild or medium case but because of the traumas and experiences that followed, Bob had the signs and symptoms of a horse that was severely herd-bound.

However, the three solutions presented in this book would probably not have worked on a permanent basis because the underlying root cause and the ensuing emotional fallout had not been resolved.

In a situation like this, you cannot hope to gain your horse's trust without solving these first. So if you have a horse that does not respond either to these or any solutions, then there is probably something else going on, something buried deeper.

This is when it's time to call in reinforcements and dig a bit deeper into what's really going on. Find the core issue. I'm always up for talking about horses and helping any way I can. So, please go to my website and book a call if you'd like some help.

My Little Secret

*"We are not human beings in search of a spiritual experience.
We are spiritual beings emersed in a human experience."*
WAYNE DYER

Now that you've reached the end of the book, I have something special to share with you...

I'd like you to ask yourself the following questions and count how many times you answer "yes":

- Have you ever known someone was going to call you just before your phone rings?
- Have you ever thought of someone and then run into them that same day?
- Have you ever felt that something was wrong with someone and then later found out you were right?
- Have you ever felt like you really needed to do something or go somewhere but you couldn't explain it? You just had to do it.

- Have you ever experienced déjà vu?
- Have you ever been around someone and you felt this uncontrollable urge to move away from them because something felt 'off'? Then after you left them you felt better?

How many yeses did you score? 3 or more? 4 or more? 5 or more?

OK, how about these questions, see how many you score with these:

- Have you ever seen a spirit? A spirit ball? Or something of that nature you simply couldn't explain?
- Have you ever lost a loved one and felt them say goodbye or felt their presence?
- Have you ever felt that someone wasn't trustworthy the second you met them?
- Have you ever just instinctively known things without understanding how?
- Have you ever felt the energy in a room change from positive to negative?
- Have you ever connected so deeply with your horse that you can shut your eyes and see what they were telling you?

How many yeses this time? 2 or more? 3 or more? 4 or more?

If you were to put a name to this phenomenon, what might it be?

Hold that thought because I'd like to tell you about an old family friend I called Uncle David.

Uncle David was absolutely amazing. I could tell you countless stories about him that would sound totally made up, but I experienced them all with him.

One time he was on a deep-sea fishing expedition in a boat off Hawaii when the boat navigation broke down. They were miles from shore and with all the cruising back and forth trying to locate the best fish, no one on board had any idea which direction they should head to get back to port.

So Uncle David sat on the side of the boat and started to meditate. After a while, he stood up, walked up to the captain, and said, *"Follow the dolphins"*.

The captain thought he was nuts, but the dolphins did seem to be just hanging around the boat so he thought he may as well give it a shot. When Uncle David said to the dolphins, *"Okay, take us home"*, the dolphins started swimming so the captain fired up the engine and followed them.

The captain and other passengers on the boat were amazed when the dolphins took them right to the island they wanted to go to! And after making their usual clicking noises as if to say goodbye, the dolphins just turned around and left. Uncle David was a very special man.

As another example of what I'm talking about, have you ever watched TV shows about wildlife in Africa? The ones that show the lions on the prowl trying to catch dinner. Have you noticed that the deer or antelope that survive seem to know instantly when the lion is in the area?

They seem to instantly know that there's something different going on, their heads go up and then they start scanning with their ears and noses for confirmation.

Do you know what it is?

It is actually something that is very near and dear to my heart and something I treasure. I know it's the reason horses are drawn to me and trust me, why they come to me for help and why they aren't afraid to be around me.

It is something I've been reluctant to discuss until recently as some people feel it's 'woo-woo' or 'hooey'. And many people are just afraid of anything that's different or strange, anything they can't explain.

However, when a horse senses it in you, he instantly knows everything he needs to know. He knows if you are trustworthy, if you have the right intentions, what your emotional state is, and if you are a threat.

Once he has all that information about you and knows he can trust you, then he will connect and communicate with you on a deeper level. Then all that's left is figuring out how to communicate properly and what the two of you want in order to be happy.

Just like in a marriage. You meet, fall in love, and start learning how to communicate with each other in a way that makes the two of you happy.

I'm sure you've seen people work with horses where it seems as if they are communicating telepathically, it's just so effortless for them.

I've heard people say that this type of communication is unattainable, or only for the most gifted or blessed. I don't believe that is true.

I believe this is a natural ability we all have; we just have to be aware of and be open to learning it.

Some students in my personal coaching program asked how they can also achieve this kind of effortless, telepathic communication and so I began to share it with them.

Now they too can see what I see and do what I do with horses because I have made these skills transferable and teachable. It's been one of the highlights of my life witnessing their transformation into amazing horsemen and women with their own magic.

As I said, I've kept this a secret for the longest time but have been urged to open up about it by these students.

You see, on the surface, my training with horses is based on my personal experiences and scientific research. The first time you go through one of my programs, you will get the results you are looking for, and that's great because that's what's supposed to happen!

The second time you and your horse go through them it takes you to a deeper, emotional level.

However, the real magic of the programs lies in the repetition beyond that, and the more times you and your horse do the exercises and the games, the deeper your understanding will become.

It's like a rose that opens more and more with each passing day until it has fully bloomed.

So what lies behind this magnificent flowering experience that awaits you?

I call it *"Tapping into the Universal Energy"*.

For those of you who didn't answer or feel like you aren't able to tap into this energy, I have two questions for you...

1. Have you ever gone to someone's house and their cat or dog comes right up to you for scratches, or the cat jumps in your lap for cuddles?

   And their owner says, *"They normally don't act like that with strangers"*.
2. Have people told you that you are good with animals?

If so, then you're already connected to this universal energy. But most people don't realize that they are connected. If you are in this category you would have answered yes to at least 2 or 3 of the questions above.

If you answered with more yeses, then you probably know that this stuff happens to you, but you may not be sure why it happens or how to turn it on or off. You just know that when you need it, it happens.

When you can deliberately tap into this energy and hone this skill, a mere twitch of your head or a shift in your seat is enough for your horse to know exactly what you're asking. And your horse is happily willing to cooperate with you. The two of you will be in perfect sync.

This connection to the universal energy links you and your horse naturally and takes your horsemanship skills to another level.

But it's even more than that though. It's an intuition, a feeling, a knowing, and a deep understanding. A way to communicate with your horse in a deeper, richer, more fulfilling way.

For those people who appear to be able to communicate telepathically with their horse, that could indeed be what they are doing, tapping into this universal energy.

Just as you want to be on the 'same wavelength' in a blissful marriage, the same is possible in your relationship with your horse. And when you are, it allows you to know what's really going on with each other and allows you to feel your way through any issues together. It makes working with your horse so much simpler.

Here's another Uncle David story...

When I got married, Uncle David came to the ceremony. Before I went into the church he came over to me and we chatted a little and then he asked me about the weather. I thought it an odd question and just said that I hoped it wouldn't rain given all the dark clouds overhead.

To which Uncle David jokingly said, *"I'll see what I can do about the weather for you.*" We laughed and then I went into the church to get married.

When we came out of the church the sky was bright blue and the sun was shining! I was of course delighted that my big day just got a whole lot better.

But towards the end of the reception, Uncle David came to me and said that he had done his best to hold off the weather but maybe it was time to take the reception inside.

It was still clear blue skies when he said this and naturally, the guests thought we were nuts to be all heading back inside when it was still sunny.

So you can imagine their surprise when 15 minutes later it quickly got dark and then suddenly started pouring with rain.

Everyone asked me how Uncle David knew. I just looked over at him and smiled, "He just does" was all I could say.

Now is a good time to tell you that Uncle David (David Nuuhiwa Sr.) was a Hawaiian Kahuna, a Lua priest, and he was nominated *"King of Aloha"* in 1959, and later *"Ambassador to Hawaii"*. He was an accomplished spiritual leader.

He was taught not only to respect all nature but to talk to her, listen to her, and learn from her. He always talked about his teachers – the birds, lizards, fish, trees, water, and wind. And that is what he taught others, how to listen and communicate with nature... the universal energy.

Uncle David could not only tap into this energy, but it naturally flowed through him. He could do and see things that other people couldn't even imagine. He could see a person's aura and tell you things about yourself that would blow your mind.

I instinctively knew to trust Uncle David and I took everything he said as gospel truth. At the time I couldn't explain it, but I knew to trust him. I knew he was connected to something I couldn't see and he was listening to something I couldn't hear. At least not at that time in my life.

I didn't think about it at the time but looking back, I guess I always did things a bit differently too, like sharing a two-way communication with animals. We just seemed to understand each other instinctually and naturally.

Being sensitive and being able to tap into that universal energy, to listen to it, to hear it, and to use it to talk to your horse is the secret to a truly magical relationship with horses because they are also a part of the universal energy.

That's what it's like for me and I absolutely know this is why horses are drawn to me and why people look at what I can do with them as miraculous.

It's also why I am able to work with hard-to-handle, shut down, and last-chance horses. The more shut down they are, the happier they are to see me. They are so excited to tell me what's been going on and have someone listen to them on their terms.

These horses know that I am connected to the same universal energy that they are and they instantly trust me. They want to be with me, talk to me, and interact with me.

I was blessed to be able to learn from Uncle David before he passed on and since then I've been able to not only hone this skill but work out how to pass this gift on to others.

I believe this is a natural ability we all have. We just have to be aware of and be open to connecting and learning how to tap into this energy and listen. Talking to your horse in a deeper, richer way is a part of this.

The real magic of my programs lies in their repetition because underneath all the mechanical training elements that most trainers teach, I have infused my programs with an extra dimension of metaphysics, the natural realm, and how to harness the universal energy surrounding us.

So the point of this chapter is to tell you that it all starts with one spark, one true connection with the universal energy around you. That ability to tap into this energy allows you to step into your horse's world simply, easily, and effortlessly. That has been my secret as to how I get the cooperation and love from my horses to fulfill my wildest dreams.

And the best news is that you can do all those amazing things with your horse too. Because I can teach you how to connect to your horse and tap into the universal energy.

Everything is possible if you believe. If you can gain this spark and develop a connection to this energy, it will all fall into place for you and your horse as well.

"I have been working with Teddie for the last 2 years. My horse is a handful. Under Teddie's expertise and guidance, I started incorporating telepathy into our relationship. It is amazing how it works. I can hear her now.

Recently my horse refused to come out of her paddock. It lasted 3 weeks until I discovered there were snowmobiles roaring in the hills around her paddock. She felt safe there.

I told her I would protect her and she will be safe with me. I then sent her visualizations of haltering her and going out of her paddock. Well, that is exactly what happened the next time I went to see her. She let me halter her and followed me out nicely. She can hear me now too."

Madeleine and Choupette

If you resonate with what I'm saying, then believe it's true, there are no coincidences. You are here for a reason. Let me help you and your horse fulfill your dreams together. You are in the right place to hear and feel it right now.

However, if you can't or don't wish to, that's fine too. You can learn the nuts and bolts of herd dynamics and herd behaviors with my programs and still develop the horse and relationship of your dreams. I'm sure you will have great success.

Thank you for your continued support to help your horses gain the happy forever life with you that they desire and deserve.

And as always... Happy Horses!

But before I leave you, I want to tell you one more story.

CHAPTER
TEN

The Missing Ingredient

"Our lives are a sum total of the choices we have made."
WAYNE DYER

I got a shock last week and it really affected me for some reason. One of my friends that I play pool with every week told me that his wife had left him after 27 years. He said that she came home and said, *"I love you but I'm not IN LOVE with you anymore."* Then she walked out, moved in with a friend and just like that, it was over.

He was shocked and couldn't even fathom what it all meant. They were friends even before they married. They have two children, one in High School and one in College. Plus they had just got back from a lovely surprise trip that he arranged for their wedding anniversary.

He said they had laughed, had fun, and everything seemed normal, he had no idea there was a problem. He has been happy for years and thought she was too. He wishes there had been some clues so he could have tried to talk them through and fix them.

He says there is nothing more important to him than his family.

This whole breakup thing shook me. I always looked at their marriage as being as solid as a rock. He has always been devoted to her, smiles when he talks about her, never complains, puts up with her stuff, takes care of her, and is a true gentle heart.

She is vibrant, rambunctious, funny, energetic (and a bit high-maintenance). But she always looked happy and was always smiling and joking around. The whole thing didn't make any sense to me, which is why it came as such a shock.

How could the relationship between two people who looked so much in love and happy, come to such a jarring and sudden end?

Apparently, his wife won't talk about it, doesn't want to work it out, and won't even take his calls. And all he wants is to have her back and he says he'd do anything to have her back, make it work and make her happy. Despite the slap in the face he's had, he's still all pure love and devotion.

What I saw in his eyes and felt in his heart was the dedication and desire that I had to find Apollo when he was taken from me.

If you haven't read that story, you will find it here...

https://teddiezieglerhorsemanship.com/apollos-return/

I recognized the same emotion in him. He is determined and IN LOVE with his wife.

Then those words kept repeating in my head *"I love you but I'm not IN LOVE with you"*.

It's really hard to explain the difference, but I totally understand what she was saying. I had two male friends and after years of being just friends both of them proposed to me at different times. I used that same line with them.

I loved them as friends and would do almost anything for them if they ever needed me. But I didn't feel that deep, heart pounding, true love that made my heart sing every time I saw them. Do you know what I mean?

When I met my husband I knew right away there was something different about him, about us. I felt happy but at a completely different level than with a friend. It's hard to explain but if you've been fortunate enough to experience it, you'll know exactly what I'm talking about.

That spark, that light, that true heart-felt joy is what brought my husband and I together. It is also what keeps us together through the ups and downs of life. I can't imagine going through this life without him by my side. However, before I met him... I thought I didn't need anyone.

Before I met him, I was happy. I had a good life, good friends, and a great family. I enjoyed my career and my life. But now, that heart-felt joy in me has increased to another level that I didn't even know existed and could never have imagined.

Just as there was a moment in time when I could pinpoint a dramatic increase in love and joy when I met my husband... there was also a moment in time when I could pinpoint a dramatic increase in love and joy with my horses. I'll never forget that moment when I truly felt connected with Jazz. And another moment when Apollo and I connected that deeply.

For each horse I have owned, there was one moment when I felt them connect. When they fell IN LOVE with me and our relationship became different. There really is an AHA moment. When I felt it with Jazz for the first time it was so powerful that I just broke down and cried. I was so shocked.

Thinking about what happened with my friends brought me back to thinking about those incredible moments in my life when I truly connected deeply to my horses and them to me. I cherish those moments.

I have discussed this topic with many of my students and the general consensus is that those moments are a rarity. But they all experience it once they go through my **Personal Coaching Program (PCP)** and open up to the spirit and energy of their horse. And I feel blessed to be able to help them create those special moments.

That deep connection, both human and horse being IN LOVE. That is the main component missing from most partnerships.

I believe it is also the missing component in almost all of the training programs that I have seen through the years.

Yes, I know you can't train someone how to fall IN LOVE with their horse and vice versa. But I can teach you the steps to a better relationship which then brings you the closeness and the ability to fall IN LOVE with each other. I bring you the opportunities to fall in love.

One of my students told me this after completing my personal coaching program:

*"One thing for sure... I know she loves me
and I know she knows I love her"*

You would not believe how big a step that was from where they started. She had always loved her horse and had done everything she could to make her happy but nothing worked. What made it even more painful was that she knew that her horse didn't really like her. So sad.

She told me she could sense there was a component missing but could never find it. Now that she has, they are IN LOVE and their partnership is incredible. She has the horse of her dreams and her horse has the human of her dreams.

Just like a marriage, you need to continuously work on it and keep the spark alive. Just because you were IN LOVE once, doesn't mean it's going to always be the same. Just as I saw with my friends who have been married for 27 years.

I am always telling my husband that we need to do things together to stay connected and sometimes we may need to re-connect. Weekly date nights, surprise adventures, flowers or cards, and maybe even a poem if it comes from the heart.

And it's not about the getting. It's about the giving.

Give what you feel in your heart, give what you want to see in your partner, give without any expectations of a return. Don't ever take being in love for granted. And the magic will happen for you too. This works for your human partner as well as your horse partner.

Fall IN LOVE all over again and watch how everything becomes simpler and easier with your horse and with your training. Add play dates, treats just to show your love, hugs and scratches filled with emotion, and just hang out together for hours doing nothing but enjoying each other's company.

Add those things to your current routine and you'll see the magic start to happen. Enjoy and be happy. I hope your horse makes your heart sing with true love and joy and vice versa.

CHAPTER
ELEVEN

What to Do Next

"Miracles come in moments. Be ready and willing."
WAYNE DYER

I hope this book will help you and your horse resolve the herd-bound issues you are currently having. I also hope that it helps you on your way to an incredible, loving, and rewarding relationship together that lasts a lifetime.

Most of my clients are horse enthusiasts who:

- Are new to horses and need help with the fundamentals and want to start off at liberty.
- Have a brand-new horse that isn't like any other horse they've ever owned and they can't quite figure him/her out.
- Know they are missing some pieces of the horse jigsaw puzzle and neither they, the programs they've bought, nor the trainers they've hired have been able to find them (like with Dave)

- Or know they are missing that special component that makes the difference between having a functional relationship and actually being IN LOVE with each other.

If you find yourself in any of these situations, here's how I can help.

I have a series of inexpensive programs to get you started and give you a flavor of my approach. You may already have some of these if you invested in some of the additional options that came with this book:

7-Day Quick Start Program – This course is designed to kick-start your confidence. Whether you've lost it completely or are just feeling unsure around horses, then this is the perfect primer to get you back on track.

Foundation of Trust – Start to gain the trust of your horse again or for the very first time. Learn to start trusting your horse again. Watch how approaching horses with a completely new mindset will transform your views on how horses operate. Learn to see the world through your horse's eyes and turn the world upside down to find solutions.

Teddie's Fundamentals - A common problem I see is the use of outdated, basic handling skills which ignore the needs of the horse and destroy any hope of a real relationship. Learn how I do the basics and how these can help you too.

Equine Qi Gong - If you're stressed and anxious around your horse, this is the perfect way to relax, take your mind off your problems, and focus on the positive energies around you with the help of a true Qi Gong Master.

<u>Beginning The Connection</u> - Watch the journey as I take a complete novice, who knows nothing about horses and is even afraid of them and transform him into someone who is confident and comfortable around horses. It will give you a sneak peek into how you can begin growing a deeper bond with your horse as well.

<u>The Stallion Series</u> - In this documentary-style video series, you will learn how easy and effective compassionate horse training can be as you watch me take two Arabian Stallions from ignored and unpredictable to happy and trusting. A masterclass in patience and love.

If you would like to set up a clinic like Dave, or learn the unique process within my *RC3 Program* online, you can find everything you need on the Learn page of my website: https://teddiezieglerhorsemanship.com/learn/

<u>Here's a quick overview to give you some idea of how my personal coaching works:</u>

1. The first thing we do is get you to learn how to start over and hit the reset button to give your brain and your horse a rest. Time to shake off the issues, the problems, the should-haves and the could-haves, and clean the slate. I teach you how to get out of the *"I can't"* and say, *"I can,"* and mean it.

2. The second thing that we do is teach you how to rebuild from nothing. I help you put the building blocks that you know, along with a few new ones, in the right place and in the right order to build a strong, trusting, and confident foundation that can withstand the test of time.

   We work directly together to personally "audit" what's working and what's not, in order to develop an easy-to-follow plan of action specifically designed for your needs and your horse.

3. The next step in the process is to work together one-to-one on a daily and/or weekly basis to fine-tune your individualized training program. This allows immediate help to correct issues and fine-tune results right away. You have direct access to me personally to resolve any issues or questions instantly.

   There's no waiting until next week or next month to find out how to fix a current issue. No remembering a question you have or trying to remember how your horse responded a week ago. You can text me immediately, and I respond right away. Or we set up a phone call the same day to talk it through. And you get to talk to me directly, not a student of mine or a student of a student.

   The fine-tuning is done immediately, and this resolves further problems that could occur if you have to wait a week or longer for an answer. As a result, progress happens more quickly and easily because of this special access and fine-tuning.

4. The last step is to walk you through a proven easy-to-follow method, a blueprint, supporting you the entire time. We go through each step together and individualize the results for your needs and that of your horse. No matter what personality, what issues, or the breed or age of the horse, we make it work for the betterment of your horse.

   I tailor the program to you and your horse to specifically address your hopes and dreams, as well as solutions to the challenges you are experiencing and your horse's core issues. This is a very personalized process to make sure that you get exactly the results you want, and I stick with you until you do.

Not only do you get access to the actual person who developed the program and who helps you along your path, but you also get someone who loves your horse almost as much as you do and someone who cares about your goals and progress and won't give up on you.

I love teaching and sharing everything I know so that my students can do exactly what I do. I teach you how to hone your instincts and become a natural horseman or woman in your own right.

Through the coaching, you will learn not only how to fix any current issues, but any and all future ones will just melt away due to the strength of the foundation you and your horse will build together.

Horses have this uncanny knack of pinpointing our weaknesses. When we can't get them to do what we want, it leads to frustration and disappointment as we lose our confidence. Soon enough, we give up all hope of realizing our dreams, and we tolerate a less than perfect partnership with our horse.

Don't let that happen to you. Everything is still possible, even if you don't believe it right now. So many times, clients have told me they'd resigned themselves to living with their issues, and then within months their horse is hanging on their every word and genuinely wants to be with them.

That can happen to you, too, so book a complimentary call, and let's see what we can achieve together:

https://teddiezieglerhorsemanship.com/book-call/

As I mentioned right at the beginning of the book, my ultimate goal is to make you as self-sufficient as possible to the point that I become the last trainer you'll ever need to go to or study with.

When I tell this to business people, they always tell me it's not a very good business model, but I don't care.

To me, it's like the story of the Wall Street banker telling the fisherman from the Caribbean how together they can build a massive fish empire that will make them so rich that they can retire to a tropical island, hang out with their buddies, drink beer and go fishing…

As Uncle David told me, this is what I am here to do. This is my gift, my life's work.

Dreams do come true, so never give up.

I wish you and your horse all the love and success in fulfilling your goals!

I want to take this last section just to say thank you to all the wonderful horses I have shared my life with. They have been such a blessing, taught me so much and shown me so much love, I will be forever grateful to all of them.

Special thanks to my feisty and brave Quarter-Horse Paint, Jazz, who was with me for 34 years...

And to my other horses…

Special thanks to Jazz's son, Apollo, my smart and gentle Quarter-Horse, who was with me for 31 years…

Special thanks to my compassionate and loving Andalusian, D'Artagnan, who passed away too young and was only with me for 9 years…

And special thanks to my little guy, Merlin, my beautiful and courageous Fresian, who is only 8 months old at this point. I know we have a lot to accomplish together and that we will continue to learn from each other for years to come.

www.ingramcontent.com/pod-product-compliance
Lightning Source LLC
Chambersburg PA
CBHW020615270326
41927CB00005B/342